SOCIAL NEW YORK
UNDER THE GEORGES
1714 – 1776

Two Volumes

The Van Cortlandt house, built in 1748.
See page 45.

SOCIAL NEW YORK
UNDER THE GEORGES
1714 - - 1776

HOUSES, STREETS AND COUNTRY HOMES, WITH CHAPTERS ON FASHIONS, FURNITURE, CHINA, PLATE AND MANNERS

By ESTHER SINGLETON

Author of "The Furniture of Our Forefathers"

Profusely Illustrated

With A New Introduction By
Ralph Adams Brown

Volume I

IRA J. FRIEDMAN, INC.
Port Washington, Long Island, N.Y.

EMPIRE STATE HISTORICAL PUBLICATIONS SERIES NO. 60

SOCIAL NEW YORK UNDER THE GEORGES   Two Volumes

First Published in 1902
Reissued in 1969 by Ira J. Friedman, Inc.
Library of Congress Catalog Card No: 68- 58928

INTRODUCTION

Nearly a quarter of a century before the late J. Franklin Jameson drew the attention of academic historians to the need for a study of social climate and condition, Esther Singleton prepared a study of the social life of wealthy New Yorkers between the accession of George the First and the outbreak of the Revolution. Published in 1902, hailed with enthusiasm by the critics of the period, this work has been long out of print and almost impossible to obtain in second-hand condition.

Illustrated with 125 excellent photographs, this more than 400-page work, in two volumes, contains a wealth of accurate and interesting information about the daily lives, customs, costumes, recreation of those New Yorkers who were in the upper economic and social brackets. The volumes are divided into the following seven parts: Aspects of the Small Town; Houses and Furniture; Table Furnishings; Costumes of Men; The Dress of Women; Amusements; Manners, Food and Culture. Each part is sub-divided into numerous chapters, thirty-three of them in all.

Miss Singleton did her research with care and thoroughness. Her sources were, she tells us, old letters and diaries, wills and estate inventories, and especially the newspapers of the period. She appears to have combed the extant files of the newspapers edited by Zenger, Gaine, Holt, Parker and Rivington with thoroughness, and thus she researched the largest and most important of New York's newspapers during this period. There are no conventional footnotes, but sources of information are often identified in general terms. The sub-title of the work tells much of the emphasis that Miss Singleton gave to her study: "Houses, Streets and Country Homes, with Chapters on Fashions, Furniture, China, Plate and Manners."

In her preface the author notes that,

> Nothing could more clearly show the life of successful activity and at the same time of luxury led by the wealthy citizens of New York than the descriptions of the houses they lived in, the contents of their various rooms, their plate, glass and china, the delicacies with which their tables were supplied, the gardens and domains in which they took their pleasure, the clothes they wore, the music they sang and played, the plays, exhibitions and shows they attended, the public and private *fêtes*, balls, dinners, and assemblies at which they gathered, and the field-sports in which they indulged. No survey of the period would be complete, moreover, without a glance at the accomplishments, tastes, and fashionable fancies and follies of the day.

Reviewing this work in the *American Historical Review*, the major scholarly journal of the time, Ruth Putnam noted that,

> A happy, self-satisfied small town, where fashion was much considered, where the round of life rolled

on comfortably and pleasantly, distances being short and social entertainment frequent, where there were nearly as good markets as in Philadelphia, almost as much education as in Boston, London modes a trifle late... such is the picture outlined in Miss Singleton's careful mosaic, put together with bits from ephemeral records. There is nothing haphazard in the author's selections. The morsels are chosen with judgment and discrimination, and so dovetailed that a fairly graphic whole is obtained. The work is painstaking and conscientious.

From the composite nature of its being, *Social New York* lacks in literary finish, but it has real value as a study of conditions. Its sturdy quality is especially grateful because there has been a plentiful crop of popular works about New York, which have handed on from one to another, a long series of half-true commonplaces and inaccuracies anent New Amsterdam and her successor, from unsifted and unweighed authorities. Better work in the field is refreshing. Moreover there is a pleasant definiteness about Miss Singleton's framework. Her picture is confined to the Georgian epoch, her figures are the well-to-do, her topic is their life and of all her treatment is effective and suggestive.

These volumes are unusual on several counts. In the first place, as noted above, this anticipated the interest of scholars in social history by a quarter of a century. In the second place, the author worked with unusual thoroughness and accuracy. Thirdly, she confined her attention to a single socio-economic class, which gives her study a unity often lacking in works of social or cultural history. Again, the inclusion of lengthy quotations from primary sources — be they newspapers, wills or letters — gives the work a strength and a tremendous interest appeal.

Finally, the illustrations are not only numerous, they are also unusual and carefully related to the text.

Miss Singleton confines her attention to the city (or town) of New York, to a single soci-economic class, and to a precise period (1714-1776). She makes valuable comparisons between conditions in New York and those in London. She also shows the relationship between fashion and custom in the two places. Furthermore, she is not afraid to generalize and to draw conclusions — witness the following:

> After having enumerated the various articles of costume and toilets and examined the contents of the milliners' and mantua-makers' shops, it is very evident that the New York woman of fashion differed slightly, if at all, from her London prototype.

These unusually valuable and interesting volumes are made available to libraries, to schools, and to the literate layman interested in the life of colonial America, through the foresight of the Ira J. Friedman Company. It should have been reprinted years ago; it may be a long time before it is reprinted again. The conclusion is obvious: this work belongs in every school and college library in the country, but expecially in those of New York State.

Ralph Adams Brown

Cortland, New York
August 1968

PREFACE

THE purpose I have had in view in the following work has been to show clearly the social conditions of the prosperous class in New York during the period sometimes known as "The Golden Age of New York," which extended from the accession of George I. till the outbreak of the Revolution. Other writers have taken pleasure in describing the humble side of life here with the Dutch *vrouw* at her spinning-wheel and the goodman on his settle at the fireside. In the following pages, this lowly side of life in Manhattan has been entirely neglected, my aim having been to exhibit the opulent and fashionable life that revolved around Fort George.

Nothing could more clearly show the life of successful activity and at the same time of luxury led by the wealthy citizens of New York than the descriptions of the houses they lived in, the contents of their various rooms, their plate, glass and china, the delicacies with which their tables were supplied, the gardens and domains in which they took their pleasure, the clothes they wore, the music they sang and played, the plays, exhibitions and shows they attended, the public and private *fêtes*, balls, dinners, and assemblies at which they gathered, and the field-sports in which they indulged. No survey of the period would be complete, moreover, without a glance at the accomplishments, tastes, and fashionable fancies and follies of the day.

This material, collected and classified in chapters, has been gathered from many sources. Old letters and diaries have been consulted through the courtesy of descendants of those who wrote them. The ordinary sources of documentary history have been thoroughly examined and sifted ; wills and inventories preserved in Albany and New York have been consulted, and in some cases complete interiors have been reconstructed by their aid. The richest mine of wealth, however, has been the newspapers of Colonial days. The publications of Messrs. Zenger, Gaine, Holt, Parker and Rivington have been exhaustively searched ; and items of news that serve to elucidate the life of the old days, and advertisements of the merchants who catered to the needs and pleasures of the community, have been carefully gathered and classified.

The picture here presented of the home of a prosperous citizen is therefore no fanciful one, since the facts as given tell their own story convincingly. This is not a book of opinions but of facts : in all cases I have endeavoured to avoid all personal prejudice and favour, and merely to reproduce the social life of the

Georgian Age with the minimum of personal comment, occasionally indicating the connection between the fashions and tastes of that day in New York and those of the mother country.

To many people, the facts here presented will be fresh and full of interest. To others, perhaps, the illustrations showing articles that were actually in the possession of old citizens famous in their day will be even more interesting. The Waltons, Ver Plancks, Beekmans, de Peysters, Alexanders, Duanes, Livingstons, Jays, de Lanceys and others, who were prominent in the mercantile and official life of the period, have left many descendants who still possess and prize useful and ornamental articles that belonged to their ancestors.

By the courtesy of the present owners, these objects have been specially photographed for this book, and many of them have never appeared in any publication hitherto. It will be noticed that among the illustrations are several portraits of social leaders of the period, and that on other pages appear articles that belonged to them. The quaint tail-pieces of the chapters are fac-simile reproductions of various advertisements that occur in the columns of the newspapers.

I have to tender my best thanks to those ladies who have kindly allowed me to illustrate my book with pictures of their precious heirlooms ; and to the

New York Historical Society, and especially to its librarian, Mr. Robert Kelby, to whose kindness I am greatly indebted for the privilege of using its priceless collections.

E. S.

NEW YORK, *October* 20, 1902.

CONTENTS

PART I

ASPECTS OF THE SMALL TOWN

PART II

HOUSES AND FURNITURE

PART III

TABLE FURNISHINGS

xi

Contents

PART IV

COSTUMES OF MEN

PART V

THE DRESS OF WOMEN

PART VI

AMUSEMENTS

Contents

PART VII

MANNERS, FOOD AND CULTURE

xiii

LIST OF ILLUSTRATIONS

List of Illustrations

xvi

List of Illustrations

List of Illustrations

List of Illustrations

PART I

ASPECTS OF THE SMALL TOWN

PART I

ASPECTS OF THE SMALL TOWN

I

THE CITY AND ITS STREETS

No city was ever more beautifully situated than New York. Commercially, also, its favourable position could not help rendering it the metropolis of a hemisphere. During the early years of its settlement, every traveller was struck with its natural beauty. Coming up the bay, whose shores at that date were abundantly wooded, the quaint little town lying at the southern point of Manhattan Island must have formed a picture that was perfectly delightful. It is doubtful if any city was ever so important commercially and politically in proportion to its size. What Goa or Batavia was to the Orient, New York was to the Western Hemisphere. Ships with manufactures and the products of the earth arrived daily from Europe and the West Indies. This little port was a great mart and clearing-house.

Its size, however, remained insignificant all through the Eighteenth Century. In 1712, two years before George I. came to the throne, the city contained only 5,816 inhabitants, of whom 970 were blacks. This number rose to 8,882 in 1731, and 21,863 forty years later. In 1744, there were only 1,141 houses; and in 1751, only 2,059. Four years later the number was 2,200. In 1766, there were 3,223, distributed as follows: East Ward, 521; North Ward, 487; South Ward, 314; Out Ward (exclusive of the district of Harlem), 270; Dock Ward, 287; and Montgomerie Ward, 664. In 1773, the city contained 18,726 whites, and 2,737 blacks.

Approaching the city, the principal front of which faced Long Island, the first building that struck the eye was the Fort, the southern end of which was built on rocks at the water's edge. It extended from the present Greenwich Street and Battery Place to the junction of Whitehall Street and Front Street. Beyond this, old prints show a cluster of quaint houses topped by a few spires, and then the ground undulates with low hills and woods in the distance. Within the Fort, lived the Governor, whose house was burnt in 1741, and again in 1773. On this site, the new Custom House is now (1902) in course of erection.

In early days, the city had been stockaded as a protection against Indians. In 1745, the dread of a French and Indian invasion was so great that a line of palisades and blockhouses was built around the northern end of the town from river to river. It was constructed of cedar logs about fourteen feet long and nine or ten inches in diameter, placed in a trench with loop-holes for muskets. The breast-work was four feet high, and four feet wide. There were three blockhouses, thirty feet square and ten feet high, with six port-holes for cannon. They were made of logs.

Aspects of the Small Town

There were four gates, or outlets, to the city : in Pearl Street, Chatham Square, Broadway and Greenwich Street. The palisades started from James and Cherry Street, ran diagonally across Duane Street and Pearl Street, and so irregularly west, south of Fresh Water and north of Warren Street.

In 1753, an enthusiastic author writes :

" With respect to what Nature has done for us there is not a happier People in the World than the Inhabitants of this Province. I have myself spent a month in their Metropolis, the most splendid Town in North America. Everything in it conspires to make New York the best Mart on the Continent. Our Coasts are regular and by a good Lighthouse might be rendered safe and easy.

" The City of New York consists of about twenty-five hundred buildings. It is a mile in length, and at a Medium, not above half that in breadth. On the South it forms a Point into a large Bay. The East side lies on a Streight which at eighteen or twenty miles Eastward opens to the Sound. It adjoins to the Hudson river on the West and such is its Figure, its Centre of Business and the Situation of its Buildings, that the Cartage in Town from one part to another does not at a Medium exceed one-quarter of a mile. The prodigious Advantage of which to a trading City is more easily conceived than expressed. It facilitates and expedites the lading and unlading of Ships and Boats, saves Time and Labour, and is attended with Innumerable Conveniences to its inhabitants."

A few more impressions recorded by contemporary visitors will help us to give a clear idea of the aspect and character of the town. In 1748, Kalm wrote :

" In size it comes nearest to Boston and Philadelphia; but with regard to its fine buildings, its opulence, and extensive commerce, it disputes the preference with them."

5

Describing the streets, he said :

" Most of them are paved, except in high places, where it has been found useless. In the chief streets there are trees planted, which in summer give them a fine appearance, and during the excessive heat at that time, afford a cooling shade. I found it extremely pleasant to walk in the town, for it seemed quite like a garden.

" The trees which were planted for this purpose are chiefly of two kinds; the water beech is the most numerous, and gives an agreeable shade in summer, by its large and numerous leaves. The locust tree is likewise frequent; its fine leaves and the odoriferous scent which exhales from its flowers make it very proper for being planted in the streets, near the houses and in gardens. There are likewise lime-trees and elms in these walks, but they are not, by far, as frequent as the others. One seldom meets with trees of the same sort adjoining each other, they being in general placed alternately. Besides numbers of birds of all kinds, which make these trees their abode, there are likewise a kind of frogs, which frequent them in great numbers during the summer. They are very clamorous in the evening, and in the nights (especially when the days have been hot, and the rain is expected,) and in a manner drown the singing of the birds. They frequently make such a noise that it is difficult for a person to make himself heard.

" Most of the houses are built of bricks; and are generally strong and neat, and several stories high. Some had, according to old architecture, turned the gable-end towards the streets; but the new houses were altered in this respect. Many of the houses had a balcony on the roof, on which the people used to sit in the evenings in the summer season; and thence they had a pleasant view of a great part of the town and likewise a part of the adjacent water and of the opposite shore. The roofs are commonly covered with tiles, or shingles; the latter of which are made of the white fir tree, or *Pinus Strobus*, which grows higher up in the country. The inhabitants are of opinion that a roof made of these shingles is as durable as one made in Pennsylvania of the *white cedar* or

6

Cupressus thyoides. The walls were whitewashed within, and I did not any where see hangings, with which the people in this country seem in general to be little acquainted. The walls were quite covered with all sorts of drawings and pictures in small frames. On each side of the chimnies they usually had a sort of alcove; and the wall under the windows was wainscoted, and had benches placed near it. The alcoves and all the woodwork were painted with a bluish grey colour."

In 1781, the traveller, Anburey, wrote :

"The city of New York stands on the southern extremity of the island, and its situation is extremely delightful; commanding such a variety of prospects, as are the most charming that can be conceived. The city is mostly built upon the East River, on account of the harbour. In many of the streets are rows of trees on each side to shelter from the amazing heats in summer. Most of the houses are built with brick, very strong and neat, and several stories high; many of them have balconies on the roof, where company sit in the summer evenings, to enjoy the prospect of the opposite shores and harbour; and the roofs are covered with shingles. The streets are paved and clean, but in general very narrow; there are two or three indeed which are spacious and airy. The length of the town is somewhat more than a mile, and the breadth of it about half a mile."

The authorities of the city were then possessed of a great deal of civic pride. They took pains to make the city beautiful and keep it neat. Many laws show this. Before examining the houses, it will therefore be well to look at a few of the ordinances dealing with streets and city life.

In 1713, an Act was passed for mending and keeping in repair the post road from New York to Kingsbridge. The road was in a ruinous condition. It was to " Be laid out the breadth of four rod and cleared the breadth of two rodd at least."

The constable had a plenty of work to do, for the city contained a considerable amount of lawlessness. It must be confessed, however, that the law's retaliation was at least as savage as the crimes that offended it. Negroes often gave trouble, though probably they were not as bad as the low piratical whites who haunted the wharves and drinking dens of New York as of any other port. Coiners and note forgers often "found how hard it is apt to go when the law and the thief have quarrels." The more humane punishments were imprisonment, ducking, whipping, pillorying, branding and hanging. In 1736, the Public Whipper was Edward Breuwen. On Jan. 15th of that year he received £2—10—0 for his quarter's salary and fifteen shillings "for sitting in the pillory, and whipping through the town at a cart's tail one Patrick Butler for issueing counterfeited dollars." Fifteen years later this official's pay was increased. In 1751, it was announced that "The Public Whipper of the City of New York being lately dead; if any Person inclines to accept that office with 20£ a year, he may apply to the Mayor and be entered."

Punishments were innumerable. Among many may be instanced the case of John Morris, who in 1768 for sheep-stealing was found guilty, but was granted the benefit of the clergy, burnt in the hand and discharged. The following year Daniel Martin received fifteen lashes for stealing fiddle strings. For defrauding and cheating, Richard Ely "was exalted on a wooden horse on a triumphal car with labels on his breast ; after which he was conducted to the public whipping-post where he received a proper chastise-

8

ment." In 1769, a certain John Jubeart, for passing
false dollars, was executed "at the stone fence," near
the city. The frail of the opposite sex were treated
with equal severity, and negroes were sometimes
burnt at the stake. The savage nature of the punishments did not always instil greater respect for the
law. On one occasion while witnessing an execution
for grand larceny a gentleman had his pocket picked
beside the gallows. From 1725 to 1756, the site of
the gallows was on the Common : in the latter year
this was removed "to the place where the negroes
were burnt some five years before called Catiemut's
Hill near Fresh Water."

Looking after the safety of the city was considered the duty of every inhabitant. In 1731, there
was declared to be a great necessity of a strong and
sufficient watch to be kept every night in New York
for the safety and peace of the said city. Therefore,
all householders in the six wards, " Being able and fit
to watch, or to find an able and fit person to watch
for him, her or them, or in his, her, or their stead, do
and ought, by reason of their habitation, occupation
and dwelling, to keep watch within the said city for
the preservation of the king's peace and for the ar-
resting and apprehending of all night-walkers, male-
factors and suspected persons which shall be found
passing, wandering and misbehaving themselves."
Of late years great numbers were declared to have
come privately into the city, some of whom were
suspected to be English convicts. Hence the necessity for a strong watch. The Act called for a
constable and eight watchmen every night, and equal

Chippendale secretary and book-case.
See page 111.

duty was to be performed by every ward in the following order : East, Dock, North, South, West and Montgomerie. No boys or servants were to be admitted as watchmen. The Negro Plot afterwards for a time made necessary military watches.

Night-hawks and Mohocks were by no means unknown in New York. They do not appear to have committed such brutal excesses as made them hated and feared in the English metropolis, but they sometimes indulged in the gentle and joyous pastime of beating the watch, wrenching off door knockers and breaking street-lamps. In 1751, a law was passed to curb the exuberance of nocturnal vivacity. It recites that sundry of the inhabitants of the City of New York, as well for the prevention of several evil practices usually committed in the night-time, as for the convenience of persons using the streets about their lawful business, are willing at their own expense to hang out lamps to illuminate the streets of the said city, but are discouraged therefrom for fear that such lamps may be broken, taken down, destroyed or carried away, or the lights therein put out or extinguished. For every such offence a forfeit of £20 was provided.

We occasionally come upon evidence of the pranks played by those Roaring Boys. Two months after the passage of the above Act, we find the following (February 3, 1752) : " Last Monday night several of the glass lamps put up about the City were taken down by Persons unknown and left whole in the Meal Market altogether. It is thought to be done by some daring Rakes, in order to convince the own-

11

ers how easy those lamps might be demolished without discovery." Another and more serious occur-
rence is reported in July, 1766:

> "Four officers sallied from a tavern where they had drunk
> too freely and near the college began to break the city lamps.
> A man who keeps a public house there happened to be up and
> leaning over his door, upon his reproving them, they gave him
> abusive language, rushed into the house, attacked him with
> their swords and wounded him in the arm. Then they alarmed
> and terrified the family and lodgers, some of whom they pulled
> from their beds. After this—they proceeded down the Broad
> Way and broke 34 lamps. Meeting the watch they wounded
> several, but one officer was arrested. The others then went
> for help and rescued their companion. The next day they
> were held under heavy bail for the Supreme Court. The pen-
> alty was £20 for each lamp."

In 1771, suggestions were made for improving
the lighting of the streets. It was recommended
that the lamps should be ten feet high and at a distance of fifty feet from one another and four feet out
from the houses, the diameter of the lamp globe being ten inches.

Among the acts regulating good order in streets
we find that in 1725, the nuisance of dogs running
loose was remedied by legislation. The Act recites
that "The butchers and other inhabitants of this city
superabound in a very great number of mischievous
mastiffs, bull-dogs and other useless dogs, who not
only run at coaches, horses, chaises, and cattle in the
daytime, whereby much mischief has ensued, but in
the night-time are left in the streets of this city and
frequently tear, bite and kill several cows and render
the passage of the inhabitants upon their lawful occa-

sions very dangerous . . . by attacking and flying at them."

In 1731, several important municipal ordinances were passed. One was intended to check mad riding through the streets by slaves as they took their masters' horses to water. If the streets were sometimes in a deplorable condition, as complaints in the papers would argue, this was not because the city fathers were indifferent. In 1731, a law declared that "the former laws of this city made for paving the streets within the same have been much neglected, whereby the citizens and sojourners within the said city are much annoyed, and the intercourse of trade among the inhabitants thereby much lessened." All inhabitants of houses or owners of lots fronting on any street, lane or alley were therefore commanded (at the expense of the landlord) to pave the walk in front and keep it in repair.

In the same year, a law was passed prohibiting any person from casting into the streets, docks, or slips, ashes, oyster-shells, or any kind of carrion or filth. People were forbidden to encumber the streets with building-material. The inhabitants, moreover, "shall on every Friday, rake and sweep together all the dirt, filth and soil lying in the streets before their respective dwelling-houses, upon heaps, and on the same day, or on the Saturday following, shall cause the same to be carried away and thrown into the river, or some other convenient place."

The law for the observance of the Sabbath in New York in 1731 prohibited servile work and buying and selling. It also forbade children, youths, maids or other persons to meet and sport, play, or make noise or disturbance. No tavern-keepers were to serve customers other than travellers during divine service or preaching. During service, two or more of the constables of the six wards walked through the several streets and lanes of the city with their staffs and took care that the law was duly observed. It was enacted " that if any children, youth, apprentices, servants, or other persons, do fire and discharge any gun, or pistol at any mark, or at random against any fence, pales, or within any orchard or other inclosure, or in any place where persons frequent to walk," the offender should be fined twenty shillings.

It was customary in those days, as now, to welcome the new year with great noise. We are told, in an Act of 1773, that great damages are frequently done on the eve of the last day of December, and on the first and second days of January, by persons going from house to house with guns and other fire-arms, and being often intoxicated with liquor they have not only put the inhabitants in great terror, but committed many mischiefs. A penalty of twenty shillings was provided to stop this.

In 1769, a law was passed inflicting a penalty of twenty shillings for firing "any gun, pistol, rocket, cracker, squib, or other fire-work, in any street, lane, or alley, garden or other inclosure, or from any house, or in any other place where persons frequently walk."

II

When Manhattan Island was first settled, it was covered with trees, with the exception of the low-lying salt meadows. Much of the timber was soon cleared away to make room for meadows and gardens, so necessary to the comfort and pleasure of the English as well as the Dutch.

What is now Exchange Place was originally called Garden Street, and this Street was again called Garden Street in 1728. Maiden Lane was originally the Green Lane. The Corporation under the English rule were always willing to have the city beautified. The inhabitants in 1708 received permission to plant trees in front of their houses. Fifty years later, trees were still a conspicuous feature of the streets.

Swamps, marshes and streams were plentiful. Broad Street was originally a marshy tract through which the Dutch had made the "Graft" or canal. At the foot, it was crossed by a bridge that gave its name to Bridge Street. At the mouth of the inlet was one of the principal landing places for vessels.

Other swampy districts that became well-known landmarks were Beekman's Swamp or Cripple Bush, and a swamp on De Lancey's estate in Greenwich village. The former was below Pearl Street and was not drained till comparatively late. William Wal-

ton's house was only about a hundred yards distant
from it. In 1734, were " To be sold 6 Lotts of Land
on the West Side of the Swamp or Criplebush, 3 of
them front the Road that leads from Spring Garden
to the Fresh Water, the other three the Street next to
the Swamp ; there is 4 good small Houses on them,
one in the Possession of Mrs. Scot."

Open spaces even within the narrow confines of
the city were not inconsiderable. Besides gardens,
there were meadows that were not occupied by
houses. Duyckinck's map of 1755 shows King's
Farm, west of Broadway, between Dye and Warren
Streets, with only " part of it layd out in plots." On
the other side of Broadway, facing the King's Farm,
was the Common, or Park, which at the northern
end was separated from the negroes' burial ground by
palisades. The latter adjoined Fresh Water, a lake
from which water flowed down both to the North
and East River. On the Common, near the site of
the present City Hall, was a powder-house. In 1725,
a gallows was also erected on the Common.

From time to time, we find complaints of en-
croachments on the common rights of citizens by
individuals. As the houses multiplied and private
gardens and open spaces were built over, the importance of common land for pasturage and recreation
increased. In 1767, a writer complaining of the high
price of milk and its adulteration thinks it arises
" from the scarcity and expensiveness of pasturage
near this City ; and this again proceeds from the late
practice of leasing out the Common Lands to people
who have large farms of their own adjoining. . . .

They afford us at a small expense earth for the red brick used in all our new buildings and if we were deprived of those lands a great advance in the price of bricks would certainly be the consequence. We should also be deprived of the stone, now much used for underpinning and other purposes. . . . They might at the common expence be put into the best order for pasture, meadow, etc., with proper enclosures and other conveniences, and keepers be hired to look after the cattle, and drive them to and from town and pasture. . . . It is also worth noting that since we are prohibited from hunting or shooting upon other men's lands, it is necessary that the citizens should have some other place for that manly diversion or exercise; otherwise they will be in danger of forgetting to use their firearms with dexterity, however necessary they may be for their own defence, and of sinking into effeminacy and meanness."

In the above communication, the allusion to the prohibition of hunting or shooting on other men's lands shows that an old grievance had only lately been remedied. In fact, only two years previously had an Act been passed to prevent hunting with firearms in the City of New York and the Liberties thereof. By this Act, a twenty shillings fine was incurred by anybody but the owner or his servants "that fires a gun in any orchard, garden, cornfield or other inclosed land, or enters into or passes through it."

" It has long been the practice of great numbers of idle and disorderly persons in and about the City of New York and the Liberties thereof to hunt with firearms and to tread down the grass, and corn, and other grain standing and growing in the fields and enclosures there, to the great danger of the lives of His Majesty's subjects, the ruin and destruction of the most valuable improvements, the grievous injury of the proprietors, and the great discouragement of their industry."

Another open space was in front of the Fort. At the beginning of the English rule, a market fair had been ordered to be held every Thursday, Friday and Saturday "att the market-house and plaine afore the Forte." Later, however, it was called The Parade, on account of the English garrison exercising here. In 1732, the Corporation resolved to "lease a piece of land lying at the lower end of Broadway, fronting the Fort to some of the inhabitants, in order to be enclosed to make a Bowling-Green there, with walks therein, for the beauty and ornament of said street, as well as for the delight of the inhabitants of this city." It was leased to John Chambers, Peter Bayard and Peter Jay for eleven years at a rent of one pepper-corn per annum.

The lower part of Broadway, being near the residence of the Governor, was always a fashionable quarter. The lots on the west side of Broadway averaged about fifty feet in width and extended back to the Hudson, which was nearer than it is now. Where is now the corner of Battery Park and Broadway, Captain Kennedy, the naval commander and collector of the port, built a fine dwelling-house in 1760, having purchased some ground on which were some small buildings for £66, from Abraham Depeyster. The Stevens, Livingston and other families followed his example, and the shady stretch reaching up to Trinity Church became known as the Mall.

A rival fashionable district was Pearl Street. One of the old houses built in the Eighteenth Century survived till very recently. Here lived Mr. William Walton, and his house and grounds were typical of many a rich city merchant of his day. It was a brick house, three stories high, relieved by brown stone water-tables, jambs and lintels. His large and fine garden extended down to the water. Another fine residence in this district was the de Peyster house, erected in 1695, in Queen Street, nearly opposite Cedar. This was also three stories high, with a balcony over its double door. Governor Clinton lived here and this house was used by Washington for headquarters. At Broad and Pearl Streets, was the famous Fraunces's Tavern, still standing.

The rich merchants sometimes had their stores and counting-houses adjoining, or in, their dwellings. Sometimes they lived in manor-houses or country-seats in the island a few miles away from the city and drove in to business. The merchants' usual business hours were from 10 A. M. to 2 P. M. In the middle of the century, Hanover Square was the centre of trade ; here were the counting-houses of Walton, Desbrosses, Borche, and other great merchants of the City ; Lewis Morris lived here, and so did the Waltons.

We find houses of all sizes on lots of varying dimensions. A few extracts from the newspapers will serve to show what kinds of houses could be bought or rented here :

" A lot of land lying on the South side of Queen's Street, thirty two Foot six Inches Front and the same in the Rear, the Length being from said Street to Low Water Mark part of the ground at the old Slaughter House." (1730.)

" A certain House and Lot of Ground, situate, lying and being in Hanover Square in the East Ward of the City of New York, now in the tenure and occupation of Mr. John Aubernau, containing in the Front, Twenty-eight foot in the Rear, Thirty-five foot; running from Hanover Square aforesaid to the Lane formerly called Drain Ditch and now The Sloat."

" The two lots of Land with the Brew-House and Malt-House thereon and a very good Well situate in Ann Street to be sold." (1732.)

" To be sold, the House and Lot of John Symense in the Broad-Way in New York, the House is as good as new, and has very good Stone-Walls; there is a small Kitchen, a Grass Plot, Wood-Yard, several Fruit Trees, and other Conveniences belonging to it, enquire of John Symense now in possession of the Premises." (1734.)

" A good dwelling-house and lot of ground North side of Pearl Street. The house is two stories high and has two rooms on a floor with a kitchen back, a gang-way on the side of it, with a large yard back bounded by the Fort Garden."

" To be let, the storehouse of Mr. Isaac Latouch's, adjoining the dwelling-house; it has a very neat warm room with a fireplace annexed to it, and is an exceedingly commodious store, with proper shelves, and well noted as a dry goods store. It would be very convenient for a batchelor." (1754.)

" A new two-story house and several adjoining lots are for sale fronting Fore Street, 44 feet and Nassau Street 46 feet. It is well built of brick and stone, has three rooms on a floor, seven fireplaces in all, spacious garret, good kitchen, fine large cellars, large entry through the middle of the house and a handsome staircase. Its situation is extremely pleasant near the Rev. Mr. Barclay's and Alderman Van Cortlandt's, where, from the chamber windows you have a beautiful prospect over the Commons and up the North River, being a seat suitable for a gentleman or merchant, having a large storehouse on the back part 40 feet long with a double door in the front, and a very fine garden, all in good fence." (1754.)

"A house and lot of ground in the Broad-Way, late belonging to Mr. Thomas Duncan, deceased, being in front, 31 feet 3–4, in rear, 41 feet 10–12, in length on the north side, 323 feet and on the south, 321 feet 1–2: from the back of the lot runs a water lot of 41 feet, 10–12 front and rear and 200 feet in length to be sold with the house: In the house are four good rooms on the first and second floors, and an entry all lined with hangings, besides a fine pantry and a bed room; also two convenient rooms in the third story, a good cellar, a cellar kitchen, underneath; to this adjoins a back building of two stories high with four convenient rooms and two cellars." The house was brick. On the bank of the river was a handsome hanging garden, with two flights of stone steps, and a summer-house at the water's edge. The yard was laid with flag stones and there were two cisterns and a pump." (1761.)

It will be noticed that the houses were not numbered. They were identified by signs. These must have made the streets look exceedingly picturesque. The signs were usually appropriate to the occupation of the tenant or owner of the house. Thus, we have John Brinner at the Sign of the Chair, a cabinet-maker. Other instances are: C. O. Bruff (goldsmith) Teapot and Tankard; James Duthie (druggist) Golden Pot; Peter Goelet (ironmonger) Golden Key; Jacob Wilkens (brass-founder) Andiron and Candlestick; Robert Boyle (pewterer) Dish; Peter T. Curtenius (ironmonger) Golden Anvil and Hammer; Joseph Cox (upholsterer and cabinet-maker) Royal Bed and Star; Thomas Brown (ironmonger) Cross-daggers; Samuel Lawrence (coach-maker) Chariot and Phaeton; Cornelius Ryan (tailor) Sun and Breeches; Jos. Stephens and Jno. Newstead (livery stable) Two Running Horses; Moses Taylor (brazier) Cat and Kettle; William Anderson (tailor) Hand and Shears, etc., etc. Other signs include the Dove and the Rainbow; Bible; Bible and Crown; Blue Ball; Golden Broad-Ax, Lock and Key; Horse and Cart; The Rose and Crown; Sign of the Two Cupids; Golden Fleece; Chariot; Unicorn and Mortar; Highlander; Chair Wheel; The Admiral Vernon; Chair Box and Carriage; Platter; Three Pigeons; Black Horse; Quadrant and Surveying Compass; Dog's Head in the Porridge Pot; St. George and the Dragon; Bunch of Grapes; King's Arms; Duke of Cumberland; Prince of Orange; etc., etc.

It was not alone the house of business that was known by its sign. Occasionally we meet with a notice such as this: "To be sold, a good brick dwelling-house in John Street, near Alderman Courtlandt's and known by the Sign of the White Bear."

It would seem that flagstaffs and vanes were rare on the buildings, or, at least, that they were worthy of special notice. For example: "John Browne, lately married the Widow Breese, continues his Leather Dresser's business in Smith's Fly near Beekman's Swamp, or Cripple Bush; at the south end of the house a staff is erected, with a Vane on the top of it."

When Kalm visited New York in 1748, he noted that there was no good water in the city; and he mentions that "at a little distance there is a large spring of good water, which the inhabitants take for their tea and for the uses of the kitchen. Those, however," he continues, "who are less delicate on this

Bedroom in the Van Cortlandt house.
See page 105.

point, make use of the water from the wells in town, though it be very bad." The spring that he refers to became the Tea-Water Pump, situated at what is now Roosevelt and Chatham streets. Here an engine was soon erected that forced the water up. This is sometimes referred to as the " Fresh-Water Engine from which the town is supplied." This was the chief source of tea-water until about 1800. The well was about twenty feet deep and was capable of producing daily a hundred and ten hogsheads, each containing a hundred and thirty gallons. The water was carted to town in hogsheads and casks. This spring was also a favourite resort and near it an ornamental garden had been laid out and called the "Tea-Water Pump Garden."

Among the wells in the city, the most frequented was that near the pond known as the Collect and the one in Greenwich between Thames and Cedar Streets near Comfort's Dock. Every morning and evening the slaves came in great numbers to fill their kegs with " Comfort's Tea-Water."

The pleasure that the inhabitants of New York took in gardens is constantly in evidence. As the town grew, it was natural that real estate in the business centre should become more valuable, and consequently that the gardens should be sacrificed and cut up into town lots. We sometimes meet with announcements like the following (1734): "To be Sold. The house, Store house and garden of Benjamin D'harriet, situate in Wall St. and several lots of ground in John St. on the West Corner of Gold St., formerly the garden of Mr. John Outman."

The gardens were laid out according to the national or individual tastes of the owners. In the early years of the century, the formal Dutch garden predominated, but as the English, French, Italian or Chinese garden came into vogue abroad, people of wealth and fashion here eagerly adopted the new styles. Advertisements of able gardeners in want of situations are plentiful, and so are offers of all sorts of flower-seeds, fruit-trees, and other necessaries for a well-appointed garden. In 1771, there is a notice of a man being killed by a summer-house, that he was moving, falling upon him. This was in the garden of a Mr. Faulkner, near Cowfoot Hill. The famous grottos of Twickenham and other English estates were imitated here. In 1765, Henry Smith, Church Street, wants to sell a fine collection of curious shells for grotto-work. In 1751, the following announcement appears :

" Any gentlemen or others desirous of adorning their gardens, Tops of their Houses or doors, etc. with Flower Pots, Incence Pots, Urns, Vases, or any other Ornament capable of being made with clay, may be supplied by Edward Annerly near the Fly Market, he having Set up the Potter's Business by Means of a Family of Germans he bought, supposed by their work to be the most ingenious in that Trade that ever arrived in America, at his Estate at Whitestone, where he has clay capable of making eight different sorts of Earthenware, a large quantity of various kinds being already made fitting to be baked, which will be soon."

The varieties of architecture, landscape-gardening, etc., most in favour in the middle of the century are shown in the following advertisement :

" Theophilus Hardenbrook, surveyor, designs all sorts of buildings well suited to both town and country, Pavillions,

Summer Rooms, Seats for Gardens, all sorts of Rooms after the taste of the Arabian, Chinese, Persian, Gothic, Muscovite, Paladian, Roman, Vitruvian and Egyptian; also Water houses for Parks, Keepers' Lodges, burying Places, Niches, Eye Traps to represent a Building terminating a Walk, or to hide some disagreeable object, Rotundas, Colonades, Arcades, Studies in Parks or Gardens, Green Houses for the Preservation of Herbs, with winding Funnels through the Wall so as to keep them warm, Farm Houses, Town Houses, Market Houses, Churches, Altar Pieces: He also connects all sorts of Truss-Roofs and prevents their separating by a new Method, and also all sorts of Domes, Spires, Cupolos, both pile and Hanging Bridges. Note: He designs and executes beautiful chimney-pieces as any here yet executed. Said Hardenbrook has now opened school near the New English Church, where he teaches Architecture from six o'clock in the Evening till Eight." (1757.)

"To be Sold or Let." (1767.)

III

HOUSE-BUILDING, FIRES, RENTS AND MAILS

THE citizen was ever in dread of fire. Houses built in the Eighteenth Century were principally of wood. The introduction of fire-engines in 1731 was due to Stephen de Lancey and his partner, John Moore. They sent to London in May of that year for two engines " with suction and materials thereto," and upon their arrival a room in the City Hall was arranged for their accommodation. They were used for the first time on Dec. 6th, 1732, when a fire broke out at midnight in a joiner's house. The report says: " it began in the garret where the people were all asleep, and burnt violently ; but by the help of the two fire-engines which came from London in the ship *Beaver*, the fire was extinguished, after having burnt down that house and damaged the next."

Within a very few years, engines were being man-ufactured here. In 1739, "A Fire Engine that will deliver 2 Hogsheads of Water in a minute, in a continued Stream is to be Sold by Wm. Lindsay the Maker thereof."

In 1731, a law for the better preventing of fire required two viewers of chimneys and hearths to see that the latter were kept clean. It also ordered every owner of a house that had three fire-places to keep two leather buckets on hand ; and one bucket, if less than three fire-places. The buckets had to be allowed out of the rent by the landlord, whose initials they had to bear. Every brewer had to keep six buckets, and every baker three. One of the frequent fatal fires was reported as follows :

" Mr. Thos. Duncan's house burnt with wife and 4 children, eldest daughter (18) saved by jumping out of a window three stories high into the arms of a gentleman who had encouraged her to this dangerous tho' only expedient. . . . The house with many valuable effects were entirely destroyed; but by the industry of the inhabitants, who are deservedly celebrated for their zeal and dexterity in extinguishing fires, assisted by the gentlemen of the army and the soldiers now quartered here, it was prevented from extending farther. One Mr. Flanagan, for being too industrious at the above fire, was committed to gaol."

The almanac of 1776 informs us that the city " Fire Engines are kipt at the Fort, four at the City Hall, one at Hanover Square, one near the Chapel, one Maiden Lane, and one at the Alms House. To manage which are one engineer, two assistants; and from each of the six wards twelve Firemen."

In September, 1749, there was a long article in the *Post-Boy* from a contributor who wished to help his fellow citizens to provide against the dangers of fire. His arguments give us considerable knowledge of the condition of the houses of the period. The majority of the roofs being shingle, the great danger of conflagration arose from flying embers from other fires. He says :

" The danger is greatly increased for want of a conveniency readily to come at every part of the roof, most houses having only a way to come at the chimney, and some even not that.

The method usually taken is to knock a hole through the roof as near the place afire as they can ; and if they have the good luck to put the fire out, yet is the house greatly damaged. In order to prevent this good servant (fire) from becoming a bad master, I would advise every man to erect a balcony over the ridge of the roof of his house.

" In extreme dry times such a place would be convenient for tubs and pails of water,—for the springs then being low and most part of the wells in the city exhausted and dry, yielding very little water at a time, a considerable stock may be got and kept ready there against a time of need. This balcony may be useful in many ways. All gentlemen of fortune and substance might keep up there, a small garden or fire engine, which costs from £15 to £20. This will enable them to keep their own roofs wet and play upon any contiguous burning house.

" They may sometimes from the tops of their houses for their own diversion, water the gardens with the water already there which by long standing in the sun would be rendered more fit for that purpose than cold water from the well. They may wash the dust from their roofs, and thereby render the water they receive into their cisterns more clean and pure. When they intend their servants should sweep their streets, they may from thence sprinkle and allay the dust. Thus by frequent use, themselves and others may become expert in working of the engines, which will also thereby be kept in good order. . . . There are above 500 persons in this city able to provide a small engine without prejudice to their estate. . . . Further, such a balcony would afford a commodious place for the observations of those versed in astronomy ; having a clear and uninterrupted prospect, freed from intervening objects. These observations generally being made at night, the curious thus employed would be as so many sentinels to discover the first breaking out of any fires in the neighbourhood, which would produce a satisfaction in any man's breast to find himself thus eminently serviceable to the public. Here a man may sometimes repair and with pleasure behold the beauties of a rising or setting sun ; and by it correct his watch or clock, and have the prospect of the neighbouring gardens, objects on the river, etc., which to some men would be no disagreeable amusement, and all without going from home."

This public-spirited citizen next has a few words to say about methods of building. We gather that the upper part of the roof had a considerable space on which a man with care could walk from end to end and side to side, but this left much to be desired in comfort and safety, for these roofs not being enclosed with rails, and having a considerable slope or descent, a man could walk well enough in the day and in dry weather, but when rendered slippery in wet or frosty weather, those who ventured there risked their lives, especially in the hurry and confusion of fire. The writer therefore recommended his fellow citizens to heed God's ordinance in Deuteronomy xxii, 8. "When thou buildest a new house, then thou shalt make a battlement for thy roof, that thou bring not blood upon thy house if any man fall from thence." He continues:

"How would it cut a man to the heart to see his friend lie bleeding in the street when he might by a small charge and reasonable care have prevented it! If a man is not utterly void of compassion and gratitude to his benefactor, or sympathy for his friend, he must needs feel a sting in his breast upon and after such an unhappy accident;—besides the great discouragement it gives others to be active on the like occasion. To the honour of the inhabitants of this city, be it spoken, that their dexterity and readiness in extinguishing of fires is singularly remarkable, and generally attended with great success, even beyond what might be hoped for.

"Upon the first touch of the fire bell, how soon do our streets swarm with men from all parts! and their willingness and expeditious behaviour has even surprised the strangers amongst us who have seen it." [The writer then proceeds to cite many instances of threatening fires that were put out with remarkable skill and bravery, and pays a handsome compliment to the firemen and authorities. He then passes on to show how a man's house may be made reasonably safe. He invokes the Legislature, first, to offer a premium to him who shall make by a limited date one thousand of the best tiles;] " also a bounty to any merchant importing any quantity in proportion to what parcel he imports. As there is plenty of clay in this province . . . in the space of six years, a sufficient quantity of tile might, by the like encouragement be procured ; especially since the breaking up of the war affords us a number of idle hands. Let me add here for information of some that know it not that several houses in this town have been tiled with very good pantiles made at Albany, as cheap as they could be had from Holland. Witness Mr. Bayard's Sugar House."

He next proposes a tax on all houses roofed with shingles, and a bounty on so much a foot for every house covered with tiles : " Roofs I say, because the gable ends of some houses are decked with shingles against N. E. storms and rains where tiles cannot be used. . . . But the flat sort of tile, such as is generally used in the City of London is preferred before the hollow sort as being easiest made and therefore cheapest." The writer goes on to draw unfavourable comparisons between the houses of his day and those formerly built here :

" The last fire in Duke Street could not have been so soon mastered had it not been for the tiled houses on each side, and a large high roof likewise tiled a little to leeward of the fire was looked on as a check. That very house would have stood but an ordinary chance to have escaped had it been shingled. Here observe the care and circumspection of our forefathers in covering their houses in such a manner as affords daily proofs of their prudence when we their sons are indolent and degenerate ;

we must praise their prudence, but our children will blame our folly." [Our reformer next suggests that if there are any objections against pantiles or flat tiles, such as the expense, or lack of time to procure them, even then Nature has sufficiently furnished us with means of security by giving us plenty of very good slate, since there are several places on the North River where there is as much slate to be had as would load a thousand ships.]

It may be that the solicitude shown by this writer for the improvement of roofing in New York is not entirely disinterested, for having reached this point of employing slate, he interpolates: "Any mason or others who desire to know the method of cutting and laying on of slate, may be informed by signifying his desire in this paper."

Next comes the question as to the means of raising the premiums to be paid for the manufacture of tiles. Five hundred pounds would probably suffice and this might be easily raised by taxing shingled houses. Besides this, there might be "a tax on coaches and chaises kept for pleasure generally by able men ; a tax on luxury and extravagances ; a duty on shingles, and other things that might easily bear it ; as an extravagance in dress in particular."

In 1761, it was enacted that houses erected in the city after Jan. 1st, 1766 should be made of stone or brick, and roofed with tile or slate, under a penalty of £50. The reason given for this law was " the frequent instances of the extensive destruction made by fire in many populous cities. . . . And there being reason to apprehend that great part of this city, from the number of the houses in the same being roofed with shingles is peculiarly exposed to the rage of that dreadful element." The enforcement of this law was, however, deferred till Jan. 1st, 1774. The reason given in 1765 was that "a sufficient quantity of slate or tile cannot at present, be had, or procured, to cover, or roof the houses and buildings that are yearly erected within this city."

It appears that the legislature adopted some of the suggestions of the above writer, for in March, 1774, it was announced that "the money arising from the Act laying a tax on dogs and cats in this city and county, passed last session, is to be given as a bounty for the making of tile for covering houses in this place." An Act was also passed regulating the size of bricks. The consequence was that in April, 1774, the papers stated that the hard sort of bricks had risen from twenty-eight to forty shillings per thousand, and the soft sort from sixteen to thirty shillings.

One of the peculiarities of early New York architecture, both without and within the houses, was the use of tiles. This especially struck Madam Knight when she visited the city in 1707. She noticed that the bricks in the houses were of various colours and arranged in patterns, and she remarked upon the tiled hearths and mantel-trees and noticed that the stair-cases were even laid with white tile. This, of course, was Dutch in origin, and the use of this form of decoration continued in many of the houses. Although we have seen the complaints that were made against the extensive use of shingles, it is manifest that some of the houses were constructed with the more solid materials. Tiles, both for roofing and for ornamenting the chimney, are frequently advertised.

In 1749, "Scripture tiles with the chapter and some plain white ones" are for sale. In 1766, John Franklin offers "a quantity of yellow brick and best blue glazed Holland roof tiles." Another advertisement of the day reads:

"Plain tyles to cover Buildings, made by Daniel Hendrickson, at Middletown Point, the same sort as are made use of in and are the Soundest and most lasting covering made use of (except the best light sort of Slate) and are generally preferable to the Boston Slate, being lighter and cheaper. No weather can penetrate if properly laid, and are the safest of any covering against Fire being not subject to fly by any heat. To be sold by J. Edward Prayor near Commissary Lakes, at the North River, New York, or by the above maker, where also may be had in the Spring, choice rubbing Bricks for uniting arches, or any Mouldings for Cornices; will also stand Fire for Ovens or Furnaces."

It has often been remarked how strangely old customs survive. The change of residence on the First of May was as usual in the Eighteenth as in the Twentieth Century. A surprising instance of this occurs in 1734, when the "printer apologizes for the shortness of the Weekly Journal, he being obliged to follow the custom of the town at May Day, and change his habitation."

Occasionally we get a glimpse of the rent required for certain houses. Thus in 1754, there is to be let "A very large house in King Street, next door to the Hon. Daniel Horsmanden Esq.; as it stood empty last year, if any good family wants it for the present year, they may have it for £20, paying the tax and keeping it in repair. It used to be let for £48 a year."

Aspects of the Small Town

Another new brick house in King Street was to be sold about the same date. It rented for £50 per annum. In February, 1764, the editor of the *Gazette* noted that he had heard there were more houses to be let in the City than there had been at any time for seven years past. It would appear that the rent question occasionally caused friction in the community. In 1749, we find an interesting address to a Hebrew who had moved into a new neighbourhood and found himself an unwelcome guest because he had made good use of his talents for business. An interesting side light is thrown on local customs in this document :

"To the Israelite of the Tribe of Judah, lately removed near Fudge's Corner.

Sir,

As it has been a custom for many years past to address new neighbours, we do out of mere form congratulate you into this our neighbourhood, but wish you may not answer the character given you by some people. We are informed you have made it a practice of late years to overbid many persons in their rents, whereby they have been put to great trouble and expense . . . . . we are assuredly informed that you was the first person discovered to be guilty of that most scandalous practice.

Alas! J———e, from the gay appearance and haughty spirit of your consort, we imagine your purse will soon be exhausted, we would therefore advise you to use proper means to prevent it before it is too late. We blame you much for hiring your now dwelling-house at so great a rent and for a term of years, when it is probable rents will fall at least one-half, we advise you therefore to pay your rent as it becomes due, otherwise the consequences may prove abortive.

It is become a custom with us to invite our new neighbours members of our club, but as we are informed you are a common disturber, we decline paying you that compliment."

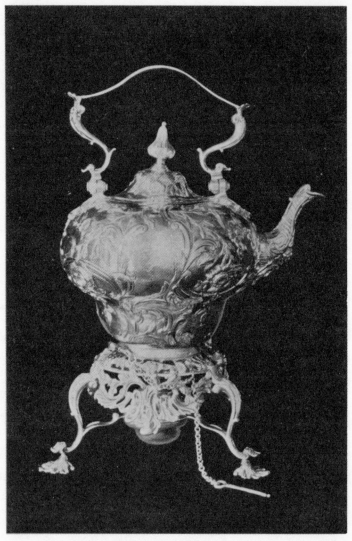

Silver tea-kettle and stand (1762–'63) owned by the Ver Planck family, now by Mrs. Louis Fitzgerald.

See page 143.

In the same year, it is announced that a number of tenants propose to form a small club contributing 6d. a piece for a ducking-stool for any one who agrees to give a higher rent than the present tenant, in view of the base prevalent practice of raising house-rents by means either of a tenant taking a house over another's head by offering a higher rent or else the landlord's baser practice of saying so, in order to raise it.

Before closing this chapter, it may be well to enumerate the buildings that existed in the city towards the end of the period under review. In 1766, as has already been stated, New York contained 3223 houses. The churches included Trinity Church, St. Paul's Church (which was not yet completed), St. George's Chapel, the Old and the New Dutch Churches, a synagogue, and churches or meeting-houses of the French, Presbyterians, German Calvinists, Seceders, or Scotch Presbyterians, Anabaptists, Moravians, and Quakers. The Lutherans also had two places of worship. Then there was the "Governor's Palace" at Fort George, King's College, the Alms House, Exchange, New Gaol, Hospital at the Battery and the Barracks.

There were five markets, known as Coenties, Old Slip, Fly, Oswego and New. Lastly, there was the City Hall. Here the General Assembly and the Council met, the Supreme Court and the Mayor's Court were held, and a public library was kept. The domestic mail service was good. The post-master of New York had a good deal of business to attend to. He frequently advertises the names of many (sometimes hundreds) of people for whom letters are lying in his office. It seems to have been a custom for him to extend credit for the delivery of these in many cases, since he sometimes announces he can give no more. The following announcement supplies us with the particulars for the year 1753 :

" The Post Office will be removed on Thursday next to the house of Mr. Alexander Colden, opposite to the Bowling Green in the Broad-Way, where the Rev. Mr. Pemberton lately lived ; where letters will be received and delivered out every day (Saturday afternoon till the arrival of the posts and Sundays excepted) from 8 to 12 A. M. and from 2 to 4 P. M. except on post nights when attendance will be given till 10 P. M. And all letters for persons living in town that remain uncalled for on post nights, will, on Monday morning be sent out by a penny post provided for that purpose.

N. B. No credit in future will be given for postage of letters."

Regular communication was kept up with England by packet-boats that plied between New York and Falmouth. The mails carried by these were made up both in London and New York on the second Saturday in every month. New York despatched mails to Boston every Monday and Thursday ; to Albany, on Monday ; and to Philadelphia, on Monday, Wednesday and Friday. The names of the Falmouth packets at that date were : *The Lord Hyde* (Capt. Goddard) ; *The Harriott* (Capt. Robinson) ; *The Duke of Cumberland* (Capt. Goodridge) ; and *The Earl of Halifax* (Capt. Bolderson).

There was a great deal of coming and going between New York and ports in Great Britain. Distinguished officials and members of the English nobility were frequent visitors. We often find notices of titled Britishers who are touring in the Colonies. A distinguished passenger list in 1769 included: the Duchess of Gordon, who had become the wife of Staats Long Morris, of the Morrisania family and had made a trip on horseback with him to the headwaters of the Susquehanna; Lady Moore; Miss Franks, Miss Burges, Miss Connor, Capt. Davis, Capt. Stanton, and about twenty others.

THE LONDON PACKET

IV

COUNTRY-SEATS AND FARMS

ATTRACTIVE and delightful as the city itself undoubtedly was, the country beyond must have been
still more charming. Manhattan Island as well as
Staten Island, the Jersey shore and Long Island were
dotted with country-seats, mansions and farm-houses
pleasantly situated in fine grounds. In many cases
these estates were comparatively small in area, as
their owners did not depend on farming for a living,
but had offices, shops or counting-houses in New
York. They could come to town by boat, or drive,
reaching their places of official or commercial business from 10 to 11 A. M. and leaving in time to dine
from 2 to 3 P. M.

The great majority of the wealthy citizens were
interested in the shipping business directly or indi-
rectly. Even if they did not build or own trading
ships, or privateers, they were generally direct importers. Everybody tried to make money, and ladies
of the best families had shops of their own. Ease
and luxury at home were cultivated, and in most
cases the mansions were situated within reach of all
that earth, forest and sea could yield. This will be
made plain by a few descriptions of this class of real
estate :

Aspects of the Small Town

"A Large Brick House well furnished (where Mr. James Harding lately lived) near New York Ferry, on Long Island, with a large Barn well covered with Cedar, a large Handsome Garden, and about Ten Acres of Land in a fine young Orchard, finely situated either for a gentleman's country-seat or a Publick House, is to be sold at a Reasonable Rate by Edward Willet, the owner thereof." (1732.)

"The plantation of the late Captain Thomas Coddrington, of 30 acres of land and two out lots of 8 acres each, orchard, dwelling-house, etc. in the bounds of Harlem, 5 miles from the town, S. E. side of the island. Plenty of lobsters and fish near the house." (1738.)

"An estate at Whitestone, near Flushing, very pleasantly situated on the Sound, consisting of a good dwelling-house, stable, chair-house, &c. with or without a large storehouse, wharf, etc., a garden of two acres walled in and well laid out with the best of fruit trees, gravel and grass walks, asparagus beds, flowering shrubs, flowers, etc., a large orchard, with mowing and pasture land." (1753.)

"A farm for sale, a quarter of a mile beyond Flushing on the road to Whitestone Ferry, containing 110 acres whereof 20 acres are in wood, and a growing swamp, lying little better than a mile from the house, 7 acres of salt meadow close by and the rest all in one body within a good stone ditch . . . . with a good and convenient dwelling-house, barn, milch, hen and pidgeon house well stocked with pidgeons; a curious flower and kitchen garden, orchard and mowing ground before the door; a well with a pump in the yard and a living spring a stone throw from the door and many other conveniences fit for any gentleman." (1754.)

"To be let May next: The farm or Plantation belonging to the Estate of Joseph Bowne, late of Flushing, deceased, containing 40 acres of choice Upland and Meadow, all in good Fence: There is on it a commodious, large Dwelling-house, furnished with nine Rooms, five of which have Fireplaces with a large Kitchen adjoining to the same; likewise, a good bearing Orchard, with a variety of Fruit trees also a good Barn, Storehouse, and other Out-Houses." (1760.)

Mr. Bayard's, described below, was a good example of an ordinary country-seat near New York in the middle of the century (1760) :

"To be let: The island called Hoobock in New Jersey, directly opposite the City of New York, lying on Hudson's River, containing between 700 and 800 acres, two-thirds of which is upland and one-third salt meadow. It is in the best order, has on it a garden of about five acres filled with a choice collection of English fruit, such as peaches, pears, plums, cherries, necterns and apricots. There is on it a very large dwelling-house, which the landlord keeps himself; and another very good one adjoining, both under one roof, which latter hires with the island; and under the whole are very large convenient cellars, together with an extraordinary kitchen. A few feet distance from the dwelling is a large new kitchen which has three rooms on each side, therefore more fitting for a family, having also the same conveniences as above mentioned; likewise the most commodious dairy for at least 30 cows.

"There are also other out-houses, as a new smoke house, fowl house, a large stable with stalls for ten horses on one side, and a fine roomly place on the other to work in when dirty weather, over which is a granary with apartments for all kinds of grain, and at the contrary end a hay-loft which will contain a great quantity of hay, besides all which there is a very large roomly barn for cows on the one side, and another for horses on the other. There are likewise on the farm a good cider mill and house over it, the loft of which will hold about 20 load of hay.

"There will be let with the premises a good wagon, cart, ploughs, harrows and farm utensils of every sort; as also 100 good sheep, among which are English rams; also 30 good milch cows and 30 head of cattle from one to four years old.

"Besides an old orchard, which in good years will produce 70 or 80 barrels of cider, there are also set out near 1,000 apple trees, all grafted with the best of fruits, some of which bore last year.

"This farm has a right in Bergen Commons, to turn out what cattle you please, and be supplied with timber for fencing and firing; is finely supplied with fish and oysters in the greatest abundance all around it, and scarce anything in America can equal its convenience for marketing, as in good weather you may cross, take one time with another, in half an hour; and in the different seasons of the year abound with plenty of wild fowl; and the farm itself all in good clover. Of the salt hay may be mowed at least 500 loads per year, and of fresh at present 60, but more may be brought. (Apply to William Bayard, living in New York). There will also be let a good pettiauger and canoe.

"The said Bayard has also on it 20 fat hogs, 6 head of fat cattle and a pair of fine oxen, besides some hundred bushels of corn, buckwheat, turnips and fresh and salt hay."

Another advertisement is of a

"Farm on Staten Island, 160 acres, house 45×37; in the Front a Dining-Room and Parlour, and in the rear, three Bedrooms, two of which have Fireplaces. The Dining-Room is 14×19, hung with genteel Paper; the Entry or Passage from the Door, is hung with the same; the Parlour is 19×26, hung with Landskip Paper framed with Papier Machee. Above Stairs are two good Bedrooms, half Story over the Front part of the house; over the back part is a large Granary divided into two Rooms. To the House is joined by a Portal or Piazza, of ten feet, a new Stone Building, thirty Feet by Eighteen. The Part next the House is finished for a kitchen. The extreme End, fronting the South, is designed for a Conservatory or Greenhouse having three Frames of Lights in the Front, containing sixty-six Panes of Glass, 9×11. Within one Inclosure next adjoining the House, is a small Orchard and Garden of about four Acres." This house was situated about a mile and a half from Johnson's Ferry upon a "Point projecting into the River, which opens a most agreeable and extensive Prospect." (1764.)

"In the Out-Ward of the City of New York, near the seat of Mr. De Lancey, called *Bloomendal*, there is to be Sold a Plantation with a very good Stone House, Barn, and Orchard, containing about four or five Hundred Apple-trees and a Pair

43

Orchard, with a great many fine grafted Pairs. The Land is very well Timbered and Watered; it has a very fine Brook very convenient for a Fish Pond, containing about Two Hundred and Sixty Acres of Land and six Acres of Meadow, situate, lying and being near *Bloomendal* as aforesaid." (1732.)

Another advertisement (1767) will give some idea of what was considered desirable in a typical house and grounds of the period:

" To be sold several lots at Corlear's Hook, about one mile from the City, now in the tenure and occupation of Edward Smith. Dwelling-house, stable, fowl-house and other necessaries; the house contains five rooms, four of which have fireplaces with a good oven in the kitchen, there is a well in the yard 36 feet deep and stoned up all the way, with a new pump. The rest of the land is laid out in a spacious garden, which the present possessor has spared no pains to render both agreeable and profitable, in it there is near 300 fruit trees all in bearing order, consisting of apples, pears, plumbs, peaches, nectarines, apricots, quinces and English cherries; all of the choicest fruit and in great variety; likewise great plenty of currants, gooseberries, raspberries and English strawberries of the different sorts; also eighteen beds of the best Battersea asparagus, in full growth for cutting, besides many thousands of puny plants fit for transplanting the ensuing season with a nursery of several thousand young trees, many of them inoculated with the best kinds of fruit; there is also 100 hills of hops which may be cultivated to good account with little trouble; likewise a root cellar 22 feet by 11 stoned up all around; also a summer house and alcove—the whole is in good board fence and is one of the pleasantest situations about the city as it commands a view of the East River and harbour from Staten Island almost to Hell Gate."

These farms or estates, therefore, were provided with all that could make life pleasant and luxurious. Gardens, greenhouses, fish-ponds, sometimes wharves, stables, paddocks, and, occasionally, deer-parks.

Aspects of the Small Town

An example of a New York Colonial country-house is shown in the frontispiece. This was built in 1748 by Frederick van Cortlandt. It enables us to form a clear idea of the average solid mansion of the period.

The islands in the bay and river formed one of the important features of the landscape. Where the statue of Liberty now stands was a pleasant and profitable spot in the old days. At one time it belonged to Captain Kennedy, afterwards Earl of Cassilis. It is thus described in 1753:

"To be Let. Bedloe's Island, alias Love Island, together with the dwelling-house and light-house, being finely situated for a tavern, where all kind of garden stuff, poultry, etc., may be easily raised for the shipping, outward bound, and from where any quantity of pickled oysters may be transported; it abounds with English rabbits."

Governor's Island, then known as Nutten Island, was both useful and ornamental. The channel between it and New York was very shallow; in fact, at low tide, cattle used to walk from one to the other. The Council set it apart as a private domain for the governor of this province. Governor Cosby used it as a game preserve. In 1738, the legislature passed an Act to preserve the breed of English pheasants in this colony. This act declares that "whereas the late Governor [Cosby] did place about a half a dozen couple of English pheasants on Nutten Island and first pinioned them to the end that they might remain there to propagate their species with a view that their increase would spread from thence and stock the country with their kind;

"And whereas, the said fowls not only have increased vastly on the said island, but many of them already spread over to Nassau Island, and in all probability will soon stock the country if people are restrained from destroying them for a few years, the present Governor being also desirous that the whole colony may be stocked with these birds," it was enacted that no birds should be killed nor eggs taken for a year. The experiment was not a success.

The first bridge connecting New York with the mainland was the King's Bridge, across the Harlem River, erected by Frederick Phillipse at the close of the Seventeenth Century. It was a toll-bridge and the charges were ninepence for each carriage ; threepence for each horse and head of cattle ; and one penny for a person. The people objected to the toll and also to the fact that the gates were locked at night. However, this was the only crossing until 1759, when Free Bridge Dyckman's was opened. This had been built by several private individuals upon Jacob Dyckman's land, a little to the south of the King's Bridge, from which the toll was lifted almost immediately.

The oldest ferry was from the present Peck Slip to the Fulton Ferry in Brooklyn, but no ferry-house was erected until 1698, when one was built on Nassau Island (Long Island), "a good sufficient house of stone and brick, forty foot in length and twenty-four in breadth, for ye accomodation and conveniency of ye persons that farmeth ye said Ferry." The "farmer" kept it as a public house of entertainment. The point where the people from Brooklyn were landed, "Burgher's Path," the "first slip," was known subsequently as the "Old Slip." Ferry-boats landed here in 1703, and also at "Countess Key" (Fly Market).

About 1732, the ferry rates between Long Island were twopence for every person and double that rate after sunset; for every horse or beast, one shilling; calf or hog, three pence; dead sheep, lamb or calf, twopence; bushel of grain, one penny; every waggon, five shillings; for every gammon of bacon, turkey or goose, one half-penny; and for every hundred eggs, three eggs.

The Ferry at the foot of the Fly Market had become so congested with boats in 1761 that it was found necessary to pass a law "that no sloop, boat or vessel, except small craft such as ferry-boats, market-boats, pettiaugers and canoes shall come within the slip." The penalty was forty shillings. This gives us some idea regarding the size of the ferry-boats.

In 1772, the city agreed to establish ferries "from Coenties Market to the landing-place of Philip Livingston, Esq., and Mr. Henry Remsen on Nassau Island; another from Fly Market to the present ferry at Brooklyn, and a third from 'Peck Slip' to land at the place last mentioned." Two years later Saint George's Ferry was provided "from a stairs directly fronting the Broad Street at the east side of the Long Bridge, and on Long Island at a stairs built at the dock of Mr. Remsen."

The slips were Whitehall, named from Colonel Moore's large house which was near by; Coenties, named for Coen and Antey (Conrad and Jane) Ten Eyck, who lived at the corner of Little Dock Street; Burling, named for the Quaker Merchant, Edward

47

Burling ; Beekman, named for the family of that name ; Peck, named for Benjamin Peck, a wealthy citizen ; and one slip on the Hudson side at the foot of Oswego (now Liberty) Street.

In addition to these, there were ferries to Powles Hook, Perth Amboy and Staten Island. Some idea of the latter may be gathered from the following announcement :

"STATEN ISLAND, 1767.

"The subscriber (John Watson) intending to remove to New York, will dispose of the Ferry and Farm he now lives on, being on the East End of Staten Island.

"In regard to a ferry, it is the best situated on the Island, as the boats can go and come from New York with most winds, and but one tide to encounter with, which is of great ease to the passengers, and is the reason that it is more frequented than any of the rest of the ferries; it has also a considerable run for carrying passengers to Long Island, which brings a handsome yearly income. Most of the shipping that goes out of New York anchors just opposite the door, being the anchoring ground for the watering-place, which makes it not only very pleasant, but of considerable advantage to the place, in carrying the passengers and ships crews backwards and forwards to New York. It also occasions a great run to the house which is the very sinew of a tavern. The boats that attend this ferry are often employed to run down to the Hook with despatches for vessels that may be there ; and the men of war which often lie here, employ them to bring their ships' stores, etc. from New York. There is an excellent dock for the conveniency of the boats ; and the best roads on the island are from this place to Amboy, the old and new Blazing-Star and Elizabeth-Town Point."

A ferry from Perth Amboy to Staten Island was provided in 1737. The rates were fourteen pence (Jersey currency) for man and horse, and fivepence for a single passenger.

Kitchen in the Van Cortlandt house. See page 161.

PART II

HOUSES AND FURNITURE

PART II

HOUSES AND FURNITURE

I

EVIDENCES OF LUXURIOUS LIVING

BEFORE 1700, New York already numbered among her citizens many rich merchants. As early as 1674, there were ninety-four burghers whose estates were valued at more than a thousand guilders each; and twenty-two of these estates represented between five and ten thousand guilders. Johannes van Burgh, Jacob Leisler and Johannes de Peyster were each worth about fifteen thousand. The other rich merchants were Cornelis van Ruyven (18,000); Jeroninus Ebbing (30,000); John Lawrence (40,000); Olaf van Cortlandt (45,000); Nicholas de Meyer (50,000); Cornelis Steenwyck (50,000); and Hendrick Philipsen (80,000).

Wealth was rapidly accumulated from the fur and timber trade and from general barter. Twelve years later, Mr. Steenwyck was worth about £16,000, an immense sum in those days. By 1700, there were a good many burghers whose estates amounted to £5,000. John Spratt (1697) with an estate of £3,779 and Col. Lewis Morris (1691) with £4,928, are instances of opulent Britishers.

53

An examination of the inventories shows that wealth and luxury were not despised. Men came here to make money, and they spent it lavishly on their homes and persons. They went richly and fashionably dressed, and their homes were provided with every comfort, convenience and ornament it was possible to procure. Their wives wore dresses of rich material and had costly jewelry; their walls were adorned with fine pictures by Dutch masters; their tables were bright with massive silver; and their rooms were full of fine furniture of English, Dutch and Oriental manufacture.

Queen Mary is generally credited with setting the taste in England for porcelains and other Eastern wares when she had shelves and cabinets fitted up in Hampton Court on taking up her residence there in 1690. Long before this, however, porcelain and lacquer ware were found in New York houses, and sometimes in considerable quantities. As the English element began to predominate, merchants of that nation grew rich in increasing numbers and

Rush-bottom and leather chairs; in the Museum of the New York Colonial Dames. See page 110.

luxury and fashion became more pronounced. The governors who came here were men of birth, breeding

54

and education, and accustomed to the best that wealth and fashion could give. Bellomont was a friend of King William; Cornbury was a Royal rake of the first order; Hunter was a wit and beau; Burnet was a friend and supporter of the House of Hanover before the accession of George I.; and all the other governors, including De Lancey, had been accustomed to the best society and familiar with kings' courts.

The picture so often drawn of the goodwife spinning in the kitchen, which forms the general living-room of the house, is therefore misleading when we are dealing with the wealthy class. The latter lived in fine houses in town with adjoining gardens, stables and offices, or had country-seats not far from the city where they were in easy reach of business. There were very few of them who were not engaged in shipping or foreign trade of some kind. They made money in all sorts of ways; farming was the least of their activities. In fact, farming on a large scale was not possible, because the area of land around their country-seats was usually comparatively small.

Take, for instance, the country-seat of Alexander Colden, Esq. It is described as "situate on Nassau Island, fronting and commanding a fine view of the harbour and city of New York. It consists of a dwelling-house and about nine acres of excellent land. The house is large and commodious, and the offices numerous and convenient. In the garden and orchard are choice collections of fruits, and of the best Newtown, Spitzenburg and other apple-trees; and towards the river on a wharf newly erected are a storehouse and boat house."

The merchants and gentry of New York were always ready for a trade venture that promised profit. It must be confessed also that they were not always over scrupulous. They would traffic with pirates and send supplies to their haunts; and notwithstanding prohibitions, they would barter firearms and fire-water with the Indians. They did not hesitate to evade the laws of trade, such as customs, when they could safely do so; and sometimes they were publicly accused of giving aid and comfort to the King's enemies by furnishing the French and Spanish with provisions, arms and munitions of war. Their privateering ventures also prospered; and the result of this miscellaneous foreign and domestic trade was that the riches, luxuries and elegances of two hemispheres were landed on the wharves of New York.

The simplest way to gain a clear idea of the interior of the wealthier homes of citizens during the Eighteenth Century is to examine a few of the inventories of men in different stations of life;—official, mercantile and professional—beginning early in the century.

Let us note for the sake of future comparison the possessions of one Cornelis Jacobs in 1700, who was worth £1953–19–3. He owned a cedar chest worth £3; six leather and six cane chairs, £6; three hammocks, £2; a chest-of-drawers, two stands and a table, £7; a walnut table, £1–10–0; three looking-glasses, £3–12–0; five pictures, £2; a whitewood bedstead with furniture, including a speckled silk coverlid, £12–7–0; a pair of brass andirons and iron frame, £1–4–0; 1 pair of andirons and 1 pair of dogs,

Houses and Furniture

£1–10–0; 1 cupboard and lignum-vitæ punchbowl, £2; a bedstead and furniture, £7–10–0; a children's bedstead and furniture, £1–10–0; a table and six old chairs, 10 shillings; a brass lamp, 3 shillings; 1 glass case, three shillings; two chimney cloths, 10 shillings; a white muslin cloth for chest of drawers, £0–7–6; and a great deal of brassware, pewter, china, earthenware and linen.

Mr. Jacobs was a good example of an ordinary Dutchman, for he had a few luxuries. His books were worth no less than £6, and his 295½ ounces of wrought plate, £103–8–6. He possessed wrought and unwrought gold equal to £32–5–0; a watch valued at £4; two East India small trinkets, £2–10–0; a "cokernut" shell tipped with silver, £1; a silver-headed sword, £3–10–0; two canes, £3; two clasped books, £2–10–0; "a chaine of pearl," £5; a feather tippet, £1–4–0; a silver box and four buttons, £0–19–3; "a china lack-

Six-legged high case-of-drawers in the Museum of the New York Colonial Dames. See page 109.

ered bowl," £0–3–0; two tortoiseshell combs, £0–10–0; and a great deal of money, some of it Arabian and Spanish. His house, kitchen and ground were valued at £300.

Turning to an English household in Queen Anne's

57

reign, let us see what Col. William Smith of St. George's, Suffolk Co., owned in 1705. He was worth £2589–4–0. To begin with, he had six bedsteads, the handsomest hung with silk and valued at £30, and three, worth £20, furnished with fine calico curtains. He had a "landskip screen," £2–10–0; a handsome chest of drawers of walnut and olive wood, £15, and two other chests of drawers, £2–15–0; one large Japanned looking-glass, £10, and two others £0–15–0; fifty-two chairs, seven of which are large elbow chairs, thirteen leather, and twenty-three cane, altogether £27–1–1 ; a number of feather beds and a good deal of household linen ; seven bed quilts, one of which was of silk and worth £8.

He owned five fine twisted rugs valued at £35 ; seventeen flannel blankets worth £1 each ; silk and other cushions, £3–10–0 ; three Turkey-work carpets and a blue cloth carpet, £4 ; a table, two comb boxes and two powder boxes, £3 ; a "silk twilite" for a table and 8½ yards of silk, £4 ; pictures worth £3–10–0 ; holland muslin and cambric, £35 ; an hourglass and two cases of knives, £1–4–0 ; six great black leather trunks, £6 ; another one, and also two large hair and three small hair trunks, £4–10–0; four large cases and bottles, £6 ; 1 case Venice glasses, £3 ; and books, £40 ; silver plate, £150 ; pewter, £20 ; chinaware, £5 ; and flint glasses, £3–14–0.

Among his miscellaneous articles, we may note a violin, worth £3 ; a fishing-rod, two screws for letters and two pewter standishes ; a silver hilted cane, £3 ; a blunderbuss and some pistols ; three swords, £8 ; a Turkey scimiter, £5–10–0 ; a large compass, two perspective glasses ; an instrument to try pearls, 12 shillings ; a loadstone and a touchstone, £2 ; and two silk colours and two drums, £15. His wearing apparel was valued at £109 ; and, in addition, he owned two seals, £2 ; 104 silver buttons, £5–10–0 ; a silver watch and gold buttons, £5–10–0 ; eleven embroidered belts, £110 ; two razor cases, and a hone, and sixteen razors, £3.

Colonel Smith was one of the residents who owned a coach, which, with cushions and harness, equaled £40 ; and a number of saddles, valued at £12–10–0, among which was a velvet saddle and a velvet side saddle worth £10.

Judging from this list of articles, even in the days of Queen Anne, when the town was amused or shocked at the pranks of her kinsman, the wild Lord Cornbury, there was considerable wealth and luxury, which had increased very greatly by the time George I. ascended the throne. Four years after the latter event (1718), Captain Giles Shelly of New York had the following household furniture. As he was a very rich man, worth no less than £6812–16–7½, it is not surprising to see that he had surrounded himself with every comfort. Among his goods, were five bedsteads. One had red china curtains ; one was a sacking bedstead with blue shalloon curtains ; one, a canopy bedstead with silk muslin curtain and white muslin inside curtain and valance ; another, with a head and tester cloth ; and the last, a sacking-bottom bedstead with a suit of striped muslin curtains lined with calico, a chintz quilt going with the latter.

He had seventy chairs : one red plush elbow, one

easy-chair, two elbow chairs, six of Turkey-work, twenty-one of cane, and twenty-seven matted, and twelve of leather. One cane couch was also among his possessions. Then there were thirteen tables: one, a small oval, one a large painted oval and one a large oval; one clock and case; one repeating clock; six looking-glasses, two pairs of sconces, one of which was gilt; a hanging candlestick; a pair of brass candlesticks with snuffers; two trays for tea; a brass lantern; "a brass hearth with hooks for shovel and tongs;" a dressing-box; two chests-of-drawers; a chest-of-drawers and looking-glass; a dog painted on a board; two warming-pans; seventy-four pictures, some in black and some in gilt frames, some black prints and "one landskip chimney piece;" five chests; three Turkey-carpets; three pairs muslin curtains and valance; four calico curtains with valance and chimney cloth; a flowered muslin toilet; a suit of calico curtains; a red and gold satin carpet; an embroidered counterpane; three pair of arras hangings; "the arras hangings from the Bowery;" four hand fire-screens a parcel of sand-glasses; a red rug; a prospect glass; and many feather beds, handsome brass hearth furniture, and pewter and copper for the kitchen.

He had a case of knives and two silver-handled knives; a chafing-dish; a great deal of valuable plate, including a tankard of 24 oz., two silver chafing-dishes and a pair of silver salts. The china included a red tea-pot, three basons, a sugar-box, twelve images and "six chaney lions." Captain Shelly owned a sword, four small arms and a trumpet. Forty-five beer glasses, a punch-bowl and a pipe of canary and some bitter wine show that he was fond of good cheer. Two pairs of tables, men and dice prove that he was fond of games; two fine coach horses, that he drove about the country in style; two patch-boxes, that he wore the fashionable *mouches* upon his cheeks; and a lot of jewelry, that he was fond of pretty trinkets. Among his curios, he had a "deer's foot tipped with gold."

As a contrast to the home of a rich country-gentleman, we may examine the belongings of Governor William Burnet, who died in 1729, worth £4540–4–3½. His home in Perth Amboy was luxurious and filled with the most fashionable articles of the day, yet some of it must have belonged to an older period, since certain pieces of furniture are referred to as "much shattered." He owned two eight-day clocks, each valued at £18; a scrutoire with glass doors, £20; eleven tables, one an oval of black walnut, another, a large one of black walnut, a third, a plain tea-table, a fourth, a japanned tea-table, a fifth, a small round table, a sixth, a card-table much shattered; and others, a square table, an oval table, and a small square table, and plain tables.

"A fine gilt cabinet and frame much shattered" must have been an unusual piece of furniture for even in its dilapidated condition it is valued at £12.

This was probably one of those handsome cabinets of the Regency, or early Louis XV. style. His looking-glasses and sconces seem to have been handsome: one is described as large with glass arms; he also had a small dressing-glass. His beds included a "coach bed with chintz curtains," worth £25; there was another with red curtains, valued at £10; and a third, an iron bedstead, with chintz curtains, worth £7–10–0. Among other articles, were a writing-desk and stand, a linen-press, a horse for drying clothes, an old chest-of-drawers, a mattress of Russia leather, a brass hearth and dogs, two old checquered canvases

Walnut chairs and writing-desk, owned by Mr. and Mrs. Benjamin S. Church. See page 65.

to lay under a table, and "a large painted canvas square as the room." The latter was valued at £8.

The Governor's chairs consisted of twenty-four red leather chairs with embowed backs, worth £28–16–0; fifteen bass bottomed chairs and a child's chair, eight walnut framed chairs, nine embowed or hollow back chairs with fine bass bottoms, £9; seven walnut chairs with fine bass bottoms, £7; two bass chairs, four ordinary chairs, and an easy chair covered with silk. He owned four pieces of tapestry valued at £20; "a fine piece of needlework representing a rustick", £5; a fire-screen of tapestry work; two paper fire-screens; and two four-leaf screens covered with gilt leather, worth £15.

The silver, china, glass and pewter, were very valuable. He had no less than a dozen silver candlesticks and "two branches for three lights," amounting, with other plate, to 1172 ounces. Three dozen silver knives and three dozen silver forks in three cases were worth another £72; his china and glass, £130–16–0; and the pewter was valued at £100–2–6. Governor Burnet seems to have been quite a collector of pictures. He owned 151 Italian prints, 20 "masentinto prints," besides numerous other pictures in black or glazed frames.

Governor Burnet's successor, Governor Montgomerie, lived no less elegantly. He established himself at Fort George, and prepared in every way to enjoy life, to make friends and to render his rule popular and brilliant. He had eight negro slaves to wait upon him and one to entertain him, a musician, worth double as much as any of the others. The Governor owned sixteen horses, a four-wheeled chaise and harness, a coach with a set of fine harness, two sets of travelling-harness, and a fine suit of embroidered horse-furniture with bridles, bits, etc., etc. His barge with its accoutrements, was worth £25 and he had a small four-oared boat. His wine cellar must have been stocked with choice vintages, since it was valued at £2500, and his library must also have been unusual, for it was estimated at £200.

Naturally, his dwelling was richly appointed. He had a fine yellow camlet bed valued at £15 ; a pair of large sconces with gilded frames, £9 ; walnut framed sconces and branches, £9 ; an eight-day clock, £8 ; a repeating table-clock, £8 ; a large looking-glass with a gilt frame, £4 ; a gilt leather screen, £3 ; twelve leather chairs, £3–12–0 ; six new black-bottomed chairs, £6 ; twelve new-fashioned matted chairs, £4–8–0 ; and six yellow chairs,—thirty-six in all ; a bed with blue china curtains ; four pairs of crimson harrateen window curtains and five pairs of yellow camlet curtains.

Among other articles were a Japanned tea-table, a pair of gilded-frame sconces, a large chimney-glass, and a walnut card-table. Two dozen knives and forks, a complete set of china, Japanned fruit plates, cut glass cruets, water and champagne glasses, and a great deal of silver. His important pictures represented Greenwich Park, a vineyard, some goats, a landscape, sheep-shearing, and a water scene. He had a parrot cage and a " Tycken " umbrella. Some of these articles and some additional ones were offered for sale shortly afterwards.

Passing over a period of ten years, we may gain an idea of a typical rich man's house towards the middle of the century,—that of Rip Van Dam, who had held the office of President of the Council and acting Governor. The house he lived in was worth about £500. It was of brick and was two stories high. The worth of his household furniture and negro slaves was estimated at from £250 to £300. Among his goods and chattels, he had a Japanned chest-of-drawers, valued at £3; a black walnut table, a looking-glass, a desk and bookcase, ten chairs, an elbow chair, (£4); a clock, (£9); a large table, a chest-of-drawers, twelve leather chairs, twelve black chairs, a mahogany table, a writing-desk, a screen, two sconces, and a backgammon table. He also owned a silver-hilted sword, and twelve gold rings. His negroes came to £50; and his silver to £90.

Two interesting chairs, whose style dates from about 1720, appear on page 62. These are walnut with high crown-backs, jar-shaped splats, cabriole legs and hoof feet. The writing-desk was given by Gen. Washington to Gen. Walter Stewart. They are owned by Mr. and Mrs. Benjamin S. Church, of New York.

"Men, women, boys and girls, to be sold cheap." (1767.)

II

LIVING-ROOMS AND THEIR CONTENTS

THE ordinary modest house of the period was of two stories with a basement. On the first floor were two rooms, used for the parlour and dining-room, occasionally divided by glass doors. Up-stairs were three bedrooms, the extra one, of course, being a small one over the hall or entry. In the basement were the cellar-kitchen and the wine-cellar. The kitchen was usually in an additional back building of two stories, the upper one reserved for the negro slaves. Frequently the house had a wing fitted up as an office.

A home of this type was occupied by Abraham Lodge who had built up quite a fortune in his twenty years' practice as a lawyer. The house was so correctly furnished that it may be taken as an example of the prosperous New York home of 1750. It was a two-story brick house with basement. The hall contained four high-backed Windsor chairs and two lanterns. From it you entered the parlour, completely furnished in mahogany. Here were eight mahogany chairs with cabriole legs and claw-and-ball feet, the seats of crimson silk damask. There was a large mahogany scrutoire and bookcase with glass-doors; a small mahogany dining-table; a round mahogany tea-table; and a mahogany card-table. A large pier-glass, a large chimney-glass, and a large gilt-framed picture brightened the walls, and the room glowed with the light of sparkling logs on the brass andirons, near which stood the customary shovel, tongs and bellows. Eleven other pictures contributed additional ornaments, as well as a great array of cut glass and burnt china ware, then extremely fashionable. A valuable treasure in this room was a casket in which the family jewelry was kept, consisting of a

Child's rocking-chair and leather-covered cradle ; in the Museum of the New York Colonial Dames. See page 78.

gentleman's gold watch, a lady's gold watch and several diamond rings.   There was also some handsome family silver.

The dining-room was scarcely less comfortable. The fireplace was furnished with brass andirons, and the light was softened by green window curtains. Here was a large mahogany oval table, a clock, ten matted chairs, a large sconce with gilt frame, two glass sconce candlesticks, a number of small pictures and all the table furniture, among which a lot of blue and white china was conspicuously displayed.

Up-stairs were three rooms. The front bedroom was the guest-chamber, and, like the drawing-room, was furnished with the greatest care in fashionable Chippendale taste. The large mahogany bedstead was unusually handsome because it had claw-and-ball feet ; its tester and curtains were of red stamped camlet, and red was the colour of the room. There was a mahogany easy chair with claw-and-ball feet and a crimson silk damask cover and cushion ; a mahogany dressing-table with drawers ; a mahogany tea-table with claw-and-ball feet and upon it a "painted table cover"; an iron bound chest and a small gilt leather trunk stood on the floor. Upon the walls hung two gilt-framed sconces, two large gilt-framed pictures, three small pictures, and two small black-framed pictures. The china in this room consisted of a large blue and white bowl and six burnt china coffee cups and saucers.

The back bedroom contained a large bedstead and a small folding-bedstead for children. The rest of the furniture comprised a small black-framed looking-glass, two black framed pictures and a small table with leaves. This sombre hue was relieved by the presence of six red leather chairs and the bright fire upon the brass andirons. Mr. Lodge had two silver-hilted small swords and walking-cane.

The third room, over the entry, was small ; and here was only an old walnut cupboard—an old-fashioned *Kas*—and a close-chair. The basement was devoted to the cellar, kitchen, wine-cellar, and storeroom.   Mr. Lodge kept four slaves, a man, two women, and a girl, who lived over the kitchen at the back of the house.   Still farther away was the stable.

Adjoining the house was Mr. Lodge's office, furnished with a writing-desk, table and stand, three matted chairs and his library.   Above this office, he had a private room to which he might retire for rest.

The Walton house, built in 1752, and which has already been mentioned, was richly appointed.   Most of the woodwork, including the staircase, was of mahogany and the furniture was of this wood.   The handsomest curtains were of silk damask, which was the material used for covering many of the chairs and sofas.   There were a number of green Windsor chairs in the house.   Some of the furniture was upholstered with the hair-seating that had then become fashionable.   There were three large walnut and gilt-framed mirrors in the house.   Mr. Walton had acquired an immense fortune in his commercial ventures and made himself exceedingly popular.   On the return of the British army from their victories in Canada in 1759, he entertained the officers in magnificent style, and it is said that the wealth displayed here was brought forward at home by some of these travellers as a proof that the American colonists were perfectly able to pay taxes for the war.   The silver that was in daily use in this luxurious home will be described elsewhere.

Another handsome dwelling was that of de Peyster, in Queen Street, near Pearl.   It gained historical interest when Governor Clinton lived there and Washington used the house for headquarters.   Abraham de Peyster, a descendant of Johannes de Peyster (a native of Holland and a merchant of New Amsterdam) and mayor of New York in 1691–'5, was possessed of great wealth.

The house that he built in 1695, and that remained standing until 1856, was situated in Pearl Street, and was a fine specimen of the rich home of the day. It was of three stories with a balcony over its generous door. The parlour, on the first floor, was furnished with a couch and fifteen mahogany and black walnut chairs and several tables: one of these a round mahogany card-table; another, a square mahogany card-table; a third, an old mahogany table; and there were also a Japanned tea-table; and two marble tables and stands. The fireplace was furnished with an iron hearth with brass handles, tongs, shovel, and brush; and near it stood a fire-screen. A mahogany desk and bookcase with glass doors and a large pier-glass completed the furniture of this room.

Upon the walls hung thirteen glazed pictures and three landscape paintings—one large and one small— and seven pictures painted on wood and canvas. Light was contributed by two glass candlesticks with branches. The windows were draped with curtains. Three cases of ivory-handled knives and forks, a case of plated ware, three china punch-bowls, a china basket and twenty china plates, and an entire china tea-service, consisting of tea-pot, cream-jug and sugar-bowl, besides cups and saucers, would seem to indicate that refreshments were served so frequently in this room that it was necessary to keep the dishes there.

The dining-room was directly behind the parlour. Here the most noticeable piece of furniture was the

large mahogany dining-table, but there were also a
mahogany tea-board and a round mahogany table.
Seven black walnut chairs with blue worsted bottoms
furnished the seats; the windows were hung with
calico curtains; and a canvas cloth was spread upon
the floor. Andirons, shovel, and tongs gave evidence
of the cheerful open wood fire. The other furniture

Chairs from the Museum of the New York Colonial Dames.
See page 109.

included a clock, a fire-screen, a pier-glass, two pairs
of sconces with gilt frames, a pair of brass candlesticks, a mahogany tea chest, and two portraits,—King
George and Queen Caroline.

In the hall were two sofas covered with leather,
five leather chairs, a dining-table and three lanthorns.
The floor was laid with canvas. At the head of the

stairs stood a tea-table, a lanthorn, and a painted wooden dog.

The principal bedroom was known as "the wainscot room." The prevailing hue was green. The bed was hung with green worsted curtains, and there were two green stools. The other furniture comprised a dressing-table and mirror, a pier-glass, mahogany stand, six black walnut chairs, two arm-chairs, an easy chair, a cabinet, andirons, tongs and shovel.

Next was the "west bedroom," and on the same floor the "tapestry room" hung with tapestry that had once been extremely fashionable but was now not much valued. The chairs here were of leather. On the same floor there was a front room used as a sitting-room. Here were two Dutch painted tea-tables, an old-fashioned pier-glass, fifteen cane seat chairs, pictures, china tea-cups, etc.

Going up-stairs, there was a "Blue Bedroom." Of course, the curtains of the bed and windows were blue. The furniture consisted of a "chest-upon-chest," six cane seat chairs, a dressing-table, a home-spun rug, a pier-glass, eight glazed pictures, and five India pictures.

Upon this floor were two other bedrooms : one, contained a bedstead with curtains, brass hearth-furniture, a looking-glass, four glass sconces, ten matted chairs, and some pieces of earthenware on the mantel-piece. In the other, in addition to the bedstead, were four matted chairs, a slate table, a square deal table, a small stand and five India pictures.

Of course, there were a garret and cellar, a wine-cellar, and an office or counting-room. In an exten-

sion were placed the kitchen and the apartments of
the negro slaves. Farther away was the stable where
were kept the horses, the chaise and the double and
single sleigh.

A good idea of the luxurious furniture of New
York in the middle of the Eighteenth Century may
be gained by glancing at the will of Mrs. Alexander,
widow of James Alexander, who died in 1760.

She bequeathed £5000 to her eldest son John, also
"my late son David's picture which hangs in the
great room above stairs:" to her son William, "my
dwelling-house with the outhouses, ground, stables
and appurtenances;" also "my largest and best carpet as also his father's and my picture." To her
daughter Mary Livingston, "all my wearing apparel
whatsoever, as linen, woollen, silk, gold and jewels
of all kinds, . . . also my chaise called the Boston
Chaise and the horse I have and keep at pasture."

To her daughter Elizabeth Stevens, the wife of
John Stevens of New Jersey, £100 "to purchase
furniture for a bed." To her daughter Catherine
Parker, " 16 crimson damask chairs, one dozen and
four crimson damask window curtains, the looking-
glass, the marble table that now are in the dining-
room, the square tea-table with the china thereon in
the blue and gold leather room, as also the one-half of
all the china and glass in all the closets, the mahogany
dining-table the next in size to the largest, the mahogany clothes chest, as also my wench called Venus
and her two children Clarinda and Bristol, also my long
silver salver, a silver tea-kettle and lamp, the chintz
bed in the large back room with the feather bed,

bolster, pillows, bedstead and furniture, . . . my third best carpet and all my pictures not given to any other . . . also £100 to buy furniture for a bed."

To her youngest daughter Susannah, £1500; also "the two large looking-glasses and the two marble tables which are placed and stand under them, the eighteen chairs with green bottoms and the green window curtains . . . in the great Tapestry Room above stairs, . . . also three sconces suiting in the above-mentioned glasses and the twelve chairs with green bottoms which are in the little front parlour below stairs, also the looking glass and pictures that hang in the old parlour below, the green russell bed and window curtains, the green silk bed quilt, two blankets, one rug, the feather bed, two pillows, bolsters and bedstead belonging thereto. . . . also the chintz bed that stands in the little back room, with the bedstead, feather bed, two blankets, one rug, one quilt, two pillows and one bolster, the large Holland cupboard, the dressing-table and dressing-glass, twelve chairs with yellow bottoms, the five pair of window curtains, the square tea-table with white china upon it which are in the room hung with blue and gilt leather, my large mahogany table and three small mahogany tables, my second best carpet, one set of blue and white china dishes and plates for a table, also a tureen, eighteen pair of sheets, 36 pillow cases, 24 table cloths, 36 napkins, 24 pewter dishes, 60 pewter plates, four of my best kettles, four of my best iron pots, four saucepans, four pair of andirons, four pair of tongs and shovels, 24 ivory handled knives, 24 do. forks, also the other half part of all the china and glass in all the closets of the house I live in also . . . my best silver tankard and two silver mugs, two pair of silver salt cellars, two sauce cups, 12 table spoons, one silver bowl, two silver tea cannisters, one sugar box, one milk pot, 12 teaspoons and a tea-tongs, one silver tea-kettle and chafing-dish, two small salvers belonging to the tea table furniture and my silver salver next to the largest." Her best horse and chaise

Mahogany dining-table, owned by Mrs. W. Sherwood Popham.
See page 111.

she gave to her daughters Catherine and Susannah equally. All other house linen was to be shared equally among her four daughters; all other plate among six children.

This was a very charming home. One room was evidently furnished in crimson damask and contained sixteen richly upholstered chairs; another room was hung with blue and gold leather; another, rich with tapestry, contained eighteen chairs with green bottoms matching the curtains; and another was in yellow, if we may judge from the twelve chairs with yellow bottoms and five pairs of window curtains. These chairs, in all probability, were of walnut, or mahogany, with the carved wooden backs. Mrs. Alexander had also some handsome beds, notably the one draped with green, the material being a kind of flowered worsted damask known as russell. She had looking-glasses and sconces in glittering frames, marble tables, and a vast amount of china and plate. The large Holland cupboard, which was, of course, a *Kas*, shows that some of her furniture was old.

Mrs. Alexander was a striking instance of the fact that in New York the keeping of a shop in colonial days did not interfere with social position. She was a woman of much energy and enterprise, and for many years had actually imported and sold goods. She was a widow when she was married to James Alexander, who was a lawyer of wealth and distinction. Their son was educated in England and while abroad endeavoured to claim the title of the Earl of Stirling. Not recognized, he returned to America where he was always addressed as the Earl of Stirling. Having noted the contents of Mrs. Alexander's home, it may be interesting to read the following advertisement that appeared in 1761 :

" To be sold at prime cost the shop goods of the late Mrs. Alexander, consisting of Broadcloths, Ratinets, Shalloons, Durants, Tammies, Worsted Hoses, Gold and Silver Lace, Silk for Women's Wear, Ribbons and China ware and a Variety of Other Goods at the House of the late Mrs. Alexander."

76

Covered jar and two beakers of Hizen ware ; owned by the Beekman family.

See page 121.

Furniture for the comfort of the children is frequently met with. We have seen that Mr. Lodge had a folding bed for his children. A child's rocking-chair and a leather-covered cradle appear on page 67. The latter bears the date 1734 in brass nails.

"Andrew Gautier, Windsor chairs." (1765.)

III

CABINET-MAKERS AND VENDUE SALES

The people of New York had every opportunity to furnish their homes handsomely. Ships brought each week the newest articles in furniture and ornament from London. Any one who had the means and took pride in living in the best taste could easily keep up with European fashions. The cabinet-makers and upholsterers were a numerous race. New artisans were constantly arriving. They had learned their trade from English cabinet-makers and were ready to make up "gentlemen's goods" at the shortest notice in accordance with the latest fashions.

Some of these cabinet-makers were undoubtedly experts; for instance, Mr. John Brinner, whose advertisement appears on page 97, was a master carver. He brought with him six artisans of ability. Any one who is familiar with Chippendale's *Gentleman's and Cabinet-Maker's Directory*, cannot fail to recognize the style of furniture that Mr. Brinner was able to make. We find him mentioning nearly every article that appears in Chippendale's book of designs, even to cases and shelves for china, furniture in Gothic and Chinese taste and the heavily draped field bedsteads.

We also find Mr. Joseph Cox making "ribband back," Gothic, and rail-back chairs, French elbow,

79

easy and corner chairs, canopy, festoon, and field-beds, burgairs, china-shelves and other articles that only a master-hand could produce.

By noting the advertisements of almost any cabinet-makers and upholsterers we can readily understand the kind of articles they made. For example, in 1750, we read :

> " James Huthwaite and Stephen Callow, upholsterers from London living in the Bridge Street, near the Long Bridge makes all sorts of Beds, Settees, Chairs and Coaches after the newest Fashion ; likewise stuffs Riding chairs and hangs Rooms with Paper and other things."

Stephen Callow "made Beds, Chairs, Settees, Suffoys, couches, and likewise hangs Rooms with stuff or Paper." In 1753, he advertises :

> " Stephen Callow, upholsterer from London (near Oswego Market), makes all sorts of beds, chairs, settees, sofas, etc., and hangs rooms with paper or stuffs in the neatest manner. He has a choice assortment of paper hangings and upholsterers' goods at reasonable rates."

Other cabinet-makers dating from 1754 to 1767 included Robert Wallace, in Beaver Street ; Thomas Griggs, near the Gentlemen's Coffee House ; John Parsons, between the New and Fly Markets near his late master Joshua Delaplain ; Gilbert Ash, in Wall Street ; and Charles Shipman, near the Old Slip. These artisans made chairs, easy-chairs, close-stool chairs, settees, couches, all sorts of cabinets, scrutoires, desks, bookcases, chests-of-drawers, and tables of all kinds,—square, round, oval, plain, "scallopt," or "quadrile." Mr. Brinner, of whom we have already spoken, who arrived in 1762, evidently did more elab-

orate work. It is quite interesting to note, however,
that there were numbers of workmen who did nothing but carve, and among these was Samuel Dwight,
carver, who lived between the Ferry Stairs and Burling Slip and did "all kinds of work for cabinet-

Chippendale chairs (1750 and about 1740).   Now in the Museum of
the New York Colonial Dames.   See page 83.

makers,"—that is to say, he carved the furniture that
they made.

In 1773, Willett and Pearsey, cabinet and chair-
makers, were at the Sign of the Clothes Press, nearly
opposite the Oswego Market, at the upper end of
Maiden Lane, "where cabinet and chair work of
every kind is punctually performed with the greatest
neatness and care."   They offered "three elegant
desks and bookcases, chest-upon-chest of drawers, one

Lady's dressing-chest and bookcase, three desks and one pair of card-tables, two sets of chairs, three dining-tables, five breakfast tables, one clock-case furnished with a good plain eight day clock, sundry stands, etc."

In 1775, Samuel Prince, cabinet-maker, at the Sign of the Chest-of-Drawers, in William Street, near the North Church in New York, made and sold all sorts of cabinet-work in the neatest manner and on the lowest terms. Orders for the West Indies and elsewhere were "compleated on the shortest notice." He had on hand for sale "a parcel of the most elegant furniture made of mahogany of the very best quality, such as chest-of-drawers, chest-upon-chest, cloath-presses, desks, desks and bookcases of different sorts, chairs of many different and new patterns, beuro tables, dining-tables, card-tables, breakfast-tables, tea-tables and many other sorts of cabinet work very cheap."

The two most fashionable upholsterers were George Richey and Joseph Cox. The former had a shop in 1759 opposite the Merchants' Coffee House, but in 1770 he was at The Sign of the Crown and Tossel opposite the Old Slip Pump. During these years he kept up with the latest London fashions and made beds, chairs and easy-chairs, couch-beds, settees, sofas, and French chairs. He festooned window-curtains "according to the latest style, as practised in London," and was always receiving from abroad paper-hangings "in the newest taste." In 1770, he made mattresses fit for sea or land and "lines and tossels to answer furniture of any colour, at the shortest notice."

Houses and Furniture

Joseph Cox was also from London and had The Royal Bed for his sign. This hung out in Dock Street and afterwards in Wall Street. He made exactly the same articles as his rival, and in 1771, put up "all sorts of Tapestry, Velvet, Silk and paper-hangings in the neatest manner." He kept a fine assortment of " lines and tossels for beds and window curtains of different colours ; " and, in 1773, offered " lines and a few very handsome balance tossels for hall lanthorns," as well as a "large assortment of bed laces, amongst which is some white cotton bed lace of a new manufactory and white fringes for ditto." In this year he advertised that he " makes all sorts of canopy, festoon, field and tent beadsteads and furniture ; also every sort of drapery, window curtains, likewise sopha, settees, couches, burgairs, French elbow, easy and corner chairs ; back stools, mewses, ribband back, Gothic and rail back chairs ; ladies' and gentlemen's desk and book-cases, cabinets, chest-of-drawers, commode dressing and toilet-tables, writing, reading sideboard, card and night ditto ; clothes presses and chests, china shelves, ecoinures, fire screens, voiders, brackets for lustres and busts, with every other article in the business."

Two styles of chairs that were fashionable throughout the period appear on page 81. These are designs that Chippendale was fond of making, and there is every reason to suppose that the New York cabinet-makers produced them in large numbers.

Apart from the efforts of the cabinet-makers and upholsterers, the merchants and importers to supply the New Yorkers with fashionable furniture and other

83

luxuries and comforts, there was still another means by which the homes of the period could be richly stocked with choice articles. Many opportunities were afforded by the public vendue, or auction. Households broke up then as suddenly as now; death sometimes removed the head of the family, but more often the British officers and those in authority were transferred to other stations and preferred to sell their household effects rather than to carry them home or move them.

Many English residents who came to America as an experiment wearied of their experiences, and before returning home sold out the contents of the house that they had taken such pains to furnish. When one remembers the custom that English people have of taking such a vast number of belongings into the wilds, it will not require much imagination to believe that when they came to New York (a comparatively easy journey), they did not hesitate to transport a ship-load of articles. Of course the Governor surrounded himself with every luxury, and at the beginning of our period, upon the death of Gov. Montgomerie, we find all his goods offered for sale at public vendue at Fort George. It may be interesting to see what kind of things he considered necessary to his comfort and pleasure, and what handsome articles New Yorkers were able to secure as early as 1731. The list reads:

" A fine new yellow Camblet Bed lined with silk and laced which came from London with Captain Downing with the Bedding. One fine Field Bedstead and Curtains. Some blew Cloth lately come from London for Liveries; and some white

Drap cloth with proper Trimming. Some broad Gold Lace. A very fine Medicine Chest with great variety of valuable Medicines. A parcel of Sweetmeat and Jelly Glasses. A Case with Twelve Knives and Twelve Forks with silver handles guilded. Some good Barbados Rum. A considerable Quantity of Cytorn Water. A Flack with fine Jessamine Oyl. A fine Jack with Chain and Pullies, etc. A large fixt Copper Boyling Pot. A large Iron Fire-place. Iron Bar and Doors for a Copper. A large lined Fire Skreen. And several other Things. All to be seen at the Fort.

"And also at the same Time and Place there will be sold One Gold Watch of Mr. Tompkins make and one silver Watch. Two Demi-Peak Saddles, one with blew Cloth Laced with gold and the other Plain Furniture. One Pair of fine Pistols. A fine Fuzee mounted with Silver and one long Fowling-Piece."

Mahogany table, owned by Mrs. Edward Parke Custis Lewis. See page 112.

Some time later we read: "At New York on Thursday, the 1st of June, at three o'clock in the Afternoon will begin to be Sold at Public Auction, a Collection of valuable Books, being the Library of his Excellency John Montgomerie, Esq., late Governour of New York, etc., deceased. A Catalogue of

the Books may be seen at the Coffee House in New
York with the Conditions of Sale." In August were
offered "several fine Saddle Horses, Breeding Mares
and Colts, Coach-Horses and Harness, and several
other things belonging to the Estate of his late Excellency Governor Montgomerie;" and on Monday
the 2d of October "about Noon, at the Exchange
Coffee House will be exposed to Sale at Publick
Vendue, a large fine Barge with Awning and Damask
Curtains; Two Sets of Oars, Sails, and everything
that is necessary for her. She now lies in the Dock
and did belong to the late Governour Montgomerie."

The negroes, plate, and furniture of the late Hon.
Rip Van Dam, Esq., offered for sale in 1749, show
that the choice goods of another governor were scat-
tered among New York houses, while in 1754 at
public vendue at the Fort were sold "sundry goods
and effects belonging to Sir Danvers Osborne, Bart.,"
—the ill-fated governor who committed suicide soon
after his arrival. These included "beds, bedding,
household furniture, kitchen furniture, pewter, turn-
ery, china-ware, a coach and harness, linen, two gold
watches, some old hock, etc., etc."

The furniture, plate, coaches and horses belonging
to the Rt. Hon. the Earl of Loudoun, also sold at
auction at Fort George in 1758, gave the residents
another opportunity of securing valuable possessions.
Captain George Douglas, Captain Thomas Seymour,
Sir Charles Hardy, Captain Plenderleath, Captain
Benjamin Davies, and the Hon. Major Carey are
among those who sold out their household goods
when they were transferred to other stations, or were

about to return to England. In addition to his mahogany furniture, Captain Benjamin Davies offered
for sale in 1775, "a fine chamber organ and a spinet."
Sometimes there were sales of objects of art. For
example, in 1771, the following pictures :

"A large kitchen with dead game, Snyders; Its companion,
do., A storm, capital, Backhousen; A Calm, Wright; A conversation, Hemskirk; Its companion; A Landskip, Flemish; A
View in Flanders, Brughel; Its companion; A Fruit Piece with
a Mackaw, Vander Moulen, together with three pairs of most
elegant vases for ladies toilet or dressing-rooms, ornamented
in the highest taste."

" Thomas Burling, cabinet-maker.'' (1774.)

IV

WALLS, PICTURES AND LOOKING-GLASSES

At the beginning of the Eighteenth Century, the walls of houses were usually panelled, painted or whitewashed. In the homes of the rich, tapestry and gilt leather hangings were found. When Kalm visited New York in 1748, he noticed that the rooms were wainscotted; that the woodwork was generally painted a bluish grey; and that the people seemed to be slightly acquainted with hangings. Two years later, wall-paper was imported in such quantities that we may feel safe in assuming it was as generally employed here as in England. In 1749, Isaac Ware noted that "Paper has in a great measure taken the place of sculpture." Furthermore, he says : "The decoration of the inside of rooms may be reduced to three kinds : first, those in which the wall itself is properly finished, for elegance, that is where the materials of its last covering are of the finest kind, and is wrought into ornaments, plain or uncovered; secondly, where the walls are covered with wainscot; and thirdly, where they are hung; this last article comprehending paper, silk, tapestry and every other decoration of this kind."

He might just as well have written this after an examination of interiors in New York. In the middle of the century, these three forms of finishing walls were found, but the latter was growing in popularity. In 1749, Stephen Callow "hangs Rooms with Paper or Stuff in the newest Fashion ;" James Huthwaite also "hangs Rooms with Paper and other Things," in 1750; and, in 1756, John Hickey "stamps or prints paper in the English manner and hangs it so as to harbour no worms."

Among the varieties of paper that are imported, we find stained paper for hangings, 1750; flowered paper, 1751 ; stamped paper for living-rooms, 1754; stucco paper for ceilings, 1760; gilt leather, 1760; and gilt paper hangings, 1765. There was also a paper with landscape views, and paper composed of pictures of the Seasons, or shepherdesses, or emble-

Wall-paper from an old house in Cazenovia ; in the Museum for the Art of Decoration, Cooper Union.

matical figures, framed in the rococo style of Louis XV. Another style, towards the end of our period, was drawn from the Classic ornamentation that the Adam brothers had made fashionable in England. A specimen of the latter appears on this page.

Generally speaking, walls were hung with pictures painted on glass, mezzotints, and engravings. Occasionally portraits were found, and in many of the houses of New York were oils that to-day would be priceless. In the inventories, quite often, a "landskip," a sea-piece, a "small winter," a "break of day," a "bunch of grapes," "a cobbler," "a plucked cock torn," an "Abraham and Hagar," a "sea strand," a "ship," "ye city of Amsterdam," suggest good Dutch art, not specially valued in that day, but commanding fancy figures now.

The fashionable pictures came from England. It may be worth while to examine the importations, remembering that Duyckinck, Rivington and Garret Noel and Company, were the chief dealers. The *Success* brought pictures on glass with gilt frames, in 1749, in which year, G. Duyckinck had "a very good assortment of Glass Pictures, Paintings on Glass, Prospective History Pieces, Sea and Landskips, a large assortment of large Entry and Stair-case Pieces ready framed, Maps of the World and in four parts, London, all on Rollers ready for hanging, Prints of divers sorts, Prints ready coloured for japanning, also a very good assortment of Limner's and Japanese colours with gold leaf and Japanner's gold dust, Silver leaf and Silver dust."

The *Neptune* brought in pictures burnt on glass in 1750; "metzotintoes burnt on glass" in 1750; "a large assortment of maps, metzotinto and copper plate prints," in 1757; mezzotints, Japanned, prospect and common prints, and "pictures of India birds and many fancies," 1759. The *Jupiter* brought India pictures in 1759; "pictures of the present King and Queen, Mr. Pitt, the Marquis of Granby; and the never-to-be forgotten Gen. Wolfe, who sold his life dear to the French on the Plains of Abraham at Quebec the 13th of September," 1762. The *Westmoreland* brought "portraits of the Archbishop of Canterbury, Dr. Seckes, Rev. Mr. Sterne, Lady Waldegrave and her child, Garrick in tragedy and comedy, metsotinto prints of Garrick and Mrs. Cibber in Jaffer and Belvidera, six very fine prints of Kew Gardens," in 1764.

John J. Roosevelt imported from England and sold at his store in Maiden Lane in 1772, "an elegant variety of pictures, one print in particular (with a very handsome frame of glass) of Regulus opposing the entreaties of the Roman Senate, importuning him not to return to Carthage. Price £14. This piece, the death of Gen. Wolfe and several others were copied from the original paintings of the celebrated Mr. West of Philadelphia." We also find advertisements that are occasionally illuminating, such as one for 1759, as follows:

"Lately published in England and to be sold by Garret Noel and Company, near the Meal Market, the celebrated Mr. Strange's very elegant Prints, consisting of Le Retour du Marche, a Cupid, a Magdalena, a Cleopatra, a Headpiece from the Painting of Guido Rheni, a Virgin Martyr from ditto, Liberality and Modesty from ditto, Apollo Rewarding Merit and Punishing Arrogance, Cæsar putting away Pompey, and Charles Prince of Wales, James Duke of York, and Princess Mary, Children of Charles I.ˢᵗ. These surprising Pieces are bound up in Boards to preserve them, but may be taken out and put in Frames. Likewise, the Heads of Illustrious Persons of great Britain, on 180 Copper Plates, engraved by Mr. Houbraken and Mr. Virtue, with their Lives and Characters by Thomas Birch, D. D., Secretary to the Royal Society. Done upon Imperial Paper and Curiously Bound. N. B. Gentlemen of Taste that are willing to purchase either of these much esteemed curiosities are desired to apply in time, as there are but very few Copies to dispose of."

Another, dating from 1760, gives a good idea of popular subjects. James Rivington of Hanover Square, had "just imported a very fine collection of Pictures of various sorts, consisting of the Heads of all the principal persons who daily distinguish themselves by their Virtues at Home or Victories abroad; of very elegant Views, Landscapes, Maps and Charts, Horses, Birds, Hunting-Pieces, Prospects of London, Amsterdam, Rotterdam, Peterborough, elegant Buildings in Poland, Prussia, the East Indies, Madrid, Lisbon, Bristol, Edinburgh, Rome, Palmyra and Athens; a complete Sett of the celebrated Beauties of Hampton Court, the Harlot's Progress, Hemkirk's Humorous Pictures, Monamy's famous Sea Pieces, Pictures for Watches, Copies to teach to Write the Round Text, the large and Small Round Hands, Black Lines, Letter Files, etc."

The feature of the room that struck Madame Knight most forcibly, when she visited New York in 1707, was the impressive fireplace with its deep hearth framed with tiles. This was generally about five feet square, and behind the fireplace was a large cast-iron and ornamented back. Sometimes they were plain, but more frequently were decorated with, perhaps, the arms of the owner, or figures, flowers, or conventional device. In 1751, we read: "Stolen out of a house rebuilding on Bever Street a small Iron Chimney back with the figure of a Parrot in a Ring on it."

China originally owned by William Denning ; now by Mrs. W. W. Shippen.

See page 127

Peter Curtenius had " some plain and figured chimney backs" in 1769.

The mantel-piece was frequently carved, as in the accompanying example owned by the New York Historical Society. It came from the Beekman House.

Tiles gave a very gay appearance to the chimney-piece. They were almost always in strong colours and the pictures were scriptural, historical, or landscape views. They were in white, green, yellow, red, blue, or purple. Marble chimney - pieces and marble hearths were also to be met with, and sometimes these were finished with a brass border. James Byers, brass founder, in South Street, said in 1768, that he could make " brass mouldings to cover the edges of marble or tiled fire-

Drawing-room mantel. From the Beekman house, Turtle Bay.

places." Once in a while, some one liked to ornament his chimney-piece, like his ceiling, with stucco-work, which Mr. Bernard Lintot was able to supply in 1760.

From the above, it will be seen that the great logs burning and crackling in their frame-work of carving, gay tiles and brass andirons and fender contributed not a little to the charm of rooms.

Although the wood fire was universal all through the period, coals also were used. "Very good sea-coal" was advertised by Nicholas Bayard as early as 1744, in which year "the newly invented Pennsylvania fireplaces" were attracting some householders, and a little before that date Franklin had invented his famous stove; and Christopher Sauer, his German device. Steel hearths and stove grates came in about 1751, and in 1752 Rip Van Dam had for sale "a large iron hearth plate with brass feet and handles." Cast-iron stoves, round and square, were also in use.

"Dutch and English fashion stoves" and "brass mounted grates with shovel and tongs" appeared in 1767; and "elegant grates, or Bath stoves, for burning coals" in 1768. Now that coals were used, the poker became a necessary addition to the equipment of the hearth. "A copper furnace and grate" was advertised in 1751.

It was not until the middle of the century that carpets became general. The word had long been used as a covering for tables, and even as late as 1771 we find an advertisement of "bedside and table carpets," showing that it was still associated with a piece of furniture. Painted canvas and haircloth were used for a long time. The latter was particularly admired for staircases and entries. It must have been the same as that used for upholstering, since Bernard Lintot imported from London in 1764 "haircloth for chair seats and staircases." Haircloth for stairs had been popular since 1750. From about 1757,

"rich, beautiful Turkey fashion carpets," as well as
Persian, Scotch and Wilton, were imported in great
profusion, and in 1771, Axminster appeared. The
carpet was kept down on the stairs by means of
brass rods.

In a period in which Chippendale and his school
flourished, it is not to be wondered at that the chimney-piece, the mirror, the cornice, the bracket, the
sconce and the girandole should
have been of the utmost
importance. At the begin-
ning of the century, the
Dutch style of carving
was in vogue; and under
the Georges, the carving,
naturally e n o u g h, conformed to the tastes that
had been formed by Grin-
ling Gibbons and his school.
Hence it is safe to believe
that New York had long supported good carvers. During
the Georgian age, they flocked
here in great numbers; and we
find many cabinet-makers who
were also carvers, like Chippendale. One of these was John
Brinner. He advertised himself as a "Cabinet and chair-

Chippendale mirror (ma-
hogany with gilded bird),
owned by Mrs. F. H.
Bosworth. See page 98.

maker from London," establishing himself at the Sign
of the Chair, opposite Flatten Barrack Hill in the
Broad-Way, his announcement reading:

Houses and Furniture

"Every article in the Cabinet, Chair-Making, Carving and Gilding Business, is enacted on the most reasonable Terms, with the Utmost Neatness and Punctuality. He carves all sorts of Architectural, Gothic and Chinese Chimney Pieces, Glass and Picture Frames, Slab Frames, Girondels, Chandeliers, and all kinds of Mouldings and Frontispieces, etc., etc. Desk and Book Cases, Library Book Cases, Writing and Reading-Tables, Study Tables, China Shelves and Cases, Commode and Plain Chest of Drawers, Gothic and Chinese Chairs; all sorts of plain or ornamental Chairs, Sofa Beds, Sofa Settees, Couch and Easy Chairs, Frames, all kinds of Field Bedsteads. N. B. He has brought over from London six Artificers, well skill'd in the above branches."

In an age of carving and gilding, the mirror received its share of attention. No one who studies the newspapers carefully can fail to note how important it was to discard an old-fashioned frame, or even shape, for the newest style of looking-glass that London had adopted. Towards the end of 1730, we read:

"James Foddy, Citizen and Glass-seller of London, who arrived here the latter end of last June, and brought with him a parcel of very fine Looking-glasses of all Sorts, and likewise appeared several times in this Paper, to acquaint the Publick that he undertook to alter and amend Old Looking-glasses; but he not meeting with suitable Encouragement, is shortly destined for the West Indies. All Persons therefore who are inclin'd to have their Glasses repair'd, or buy new, may apply to the said James Foddy at Mr. Verplanck's in New York."

By 1735, there were some new styles. Mr. Duyck-inck informed the public that he had

"Looking-glasses new silvered and the Frames plaine Japan'd or Flowered, also all sorts of Picktures made and sold, all manner of painting work done. Likewise Looking-glasses and all sorts of painting Coullers and Oyl sold at reasonable Rates by Girardus Duyckinck, at the Sign of the Two Cupids, near the Old Slip Market.

" N. B. Where you may have ready Money for old Looking-Glasses."

Looking-glasses, of course, included the large
glass that so frequently ornamented the chimney-
piece, the tall pier-glass whose place was between the
windows, and the concave and convex mirrors with
sconces for candles that were hung upon the walls.
Frequently the frames of these were richly carved
and gilded, and from the candlesticks hung glittering
drops of glass, known as girandoles. Mahogany and
black walnut were also used for frames, and a mahogany or walnut frame, brightened with gilt edges
and adorned with some carved and gilded ornament,
was also popular. One of the latter appears on page
96 ; and another on page 324. The former is ornamented with a gilded bird,—one of Chippendale's
favourite designs. This belongs to Mrs. F. H. Bosworth. The second, now belonging to Mrs. Wilmot
Townsend Cox, was originally owned by Rutger
Bleecker.

In 1769, one Minshall, carver and gilder, from
London, lived in Dock Street, opposite Bolton and
Sigell's Tavern, where he had " carved frames for
glasses, picture frames, tables, chairs, girondoles,
chimney - pieces, brackets, candlestands, clock and
watch cases, bed and window cornicing. He makes
Paper ornaments for Ceilings and Stair-cases in the
present mode." In the same year Nicholas Bernard,
carver, advertised :

" A neat assortment of Looking-glasses in the most elegant
and newest Fashions, with carved, and carved and gilt frames,
do. pediments and plain mahogany and walnut, also Dressing-

glasses, Girondelles, Chimney-Pieces, Figures of Plaster of Paris, and Paper Machine for Ceilings; the King's Coat-of-Arms neatly carved, fit for Church or public Building."

In 1775, the above Minshall, who for some time had had a Looking-Glass Store, removed it from Smith Street to Hanover Square (opposite Mr. Goelet's Sign of the Golden Key), and told his customers that he had "an elegant assortment of looking-glasses in oval and square ornamental frames." He also had some in mahogany frames and " the greatest variety of girandoles ever imported to this city." He had "an elegant assortment of frames without glass " and " any Lady or Gentleman that have glass in old-fashioned frames may have them cut to ovals, or put in any pattern that pleases them best." The frames could be finished " white, or green and white, purple, or any other colour that suits the furniture of the room, or gilt in oil or burnished gold equal to the best imported." An Apprentice was wanted "to learn the above art of Carving and Gilding ; none need apply but those who have a lad of sober and promising genius and are willing to give a premium."

The following partial list of importations may be of interest to illustrate the large general demand for mirrors : Gilt and plain looking-glasses and sconces of sundry sizes, in 1745 ; "a parcel of very fine large and small looking - glasses," 1747 ; japanned dressing-glasses, 1748 ; new fashion sconces and looking-glasses, 1749 ; looking-glass sconces, 1750 ; gilt and plain looking-glasses of sundry sizes, 1751 ; a choice assortment of very handsome looking-glasses, sconces and pier glasses of all sizes, 1752 ; a neat

Iron tea tray decorated with oil painting in imitation of Joseph Vernet; in the Museum for the Art of Decoration, Cooper Union. See page 112.

assortment of sconces gilt and carved in the newest fashions, 1753; ladies fine dressing gilt looking-glasses and small pocket ditto, 1755; "peer" and sconce looking - glasses, 1757; newest fashioned looking-glasses from London, 1757; a variety of sconces with branches in walnut frames with gilt edges, 1757; neat dressing-glasses for ladies with gilt frames, 1757; a raree-show of looking-glasses, 1758; a few handsome sconces, 1758; looking-glasses, pier and sconce, plain and gilt frames, 1758; camp looking-glasses, 1759; walnut framed looking-glasses, 1759; a good assortment of small black walnut frame and japanned looking-glasses, 1758; a large and neat assortment of dressing-sconces and looking-glasses, 1759; a very fine assortment of looking-glasses and sconces, their frames in the most genteel and richest taste, 1760; a quantity of Indian and Guinea looking-glasses, 1761; French pocket looking-glasses, 1761; looking-glasses framed in the newest taste £8 to £30 a piece, 1761; a new and large assortment of looking-glasses, sconces and dressing-glasses, 1761; looking-glasses from 2 to 6 feet, 1764; "the largest and most curious collection of plain and ornamented looking-glasses and pictures ever imported to America," 1764; convex and concave mirrors, 1764; two carved white-framed sconce glasses, 1764; handsome pier glass and two sconces with gilt frame, 1768; large pier glass in an elegant carved frame, 1769; looking-glasses from 2 shillings to £10, 1771; painted frame looking-glasses, 1773; oval sconces with gilt frames, 1773; oval glasses, pier glasses and sconces in burnished gold, glass bordered, mahogany and black walnut frames with

gilt ornaments of all sizes, likewise elegant girandoles, 1774.

People prized these articles very highly, as will be
seen from the following advertisement in 1775 :

"Stolen in the night of the 5th inst. out of the house of
Robert Murray, at Inklinbergh, a Looking-Glass, three feet
and a half long and twenty inches broad, set in a mahogany
frame with a narrow gilt edge. Whoever brings the said glass
to the owner, shall have Forty Shillings as a reward : and if
the thief be taken and convicted, a further sum of Eight
Pounds by Robert Murray."

A square or round lantern always hung in the
hall or entry, and sometimes a second one was re-
peated at the landing. There were also glass lamps
and chamber lamps, and lamps for sick persons.

The King's Arms. (1767.)

V

THE bed was, of course, the most important piece of furniture in the bedroom. Almost invariably, it was a tall and wide four-poster of mahogany, more or less richly carved. But the framework, handsome as it might be, and even if crowned by a carved tester, was comparatively unimportant when the furnishings are remembered. A large feather bed, weighing many pounds and stuffed with the softest feathers, rested upon a simple arrangement of bed-cords, or a "sacking-bottom,"—a kind of heavy sail-cloth from which the word "bed-bunt" was probably derived. "Bed-bunts" were imported and were usually 6 × 4 ft. and 9 × 4 ft., which shows the average size of the bed.

The sheeting usually came from Holland, and was known as "ozenbrigs;" the blankets were "striped," "rose," or "swanskin;" and the spreads, or "sprees," early in the century were "white cotton bed carpets," but they were supplanted later by "white flowered counterpains." Marseilles quilts came in about 1772. India chintz counterpanes were also used in 1768, and scarlet, blue, flowered, and black figured "drawboys" in 1771. A silk quilt, or a Turkey quilt, was usually folded neatly and laid across the foot of the bed. The bolster and pillows, stuffed with softest feathers,

103

were encased in white linen, and everything about the bed invited repose.

The true glory of the bed, however, was its hangings. Not infrequently, they were very luxurious in

Chair and double corner-chair ; in the Museum of the New York
Colonial Dames.   See page 109.

texture and rich in colour.   A "yellow silk damask bed," a "yellow camlet laced," a "crimson harrateen," a "green russell," a "crimson moreen," a "flowered russell," a "blue and green flowered russell," or "a green silk and worsted damask," was generally to be met with in the richest homes.   Sometimes the curtains were altogether of silk damask; sometimes, of worsted damask lined with silk; sometimes a mixture of each; and sometimes of purely woollen goods.

Occasionally, these curtains were ornamented with "silk bed lace," or fringe, or gimp, or "snail trimming," a kind of braid arranged in symmetrical rolled-up patterns, that was exceedingly popular with the upholsterers of the day, who were called upon to arrange the festoons and rosettes, lines and tassels, according to the latest advices from London. The curtains at the windows always matched the bed-hangings, and gave the room its designation of "the yellow room," "the blue room," "the red room," or "the green room." In summer, these rich hangings were removed, and the beds were draped in white, or supplied with mosquito netting, or "catgut gauze."

In some of the rooms, the beds were simpler, such as, for example, the one seen in the illustration on page 23, showing an excellent bedroom of the period, from the Museum of the New York Colonial Dames at Van Cortlandt. The simpler bedsteads were of maple or walnut, instead of mahogany, and perhaps, indeed, of pine or white-wood, stained or painted. These were hung with coloured calico curtains, like the one referred to, bright-hued or flowered chintz, or figured dimity. Ships were constantly bringing over such varieties of attractive English and India chintzes, and calicoes of such multitudinous colours and patterns, with "lines and tossels to match," that we can readily believe the bedrooms were anything but monotonous in colour and effect, even if the same arrangement of furniture was to be found in every home.

About 1770, a new style of bed and window curtain was introduced from England,—"copper plate and pencilled furniture" in red and white, blue and white, purple and white, green and white, etc., etc., so called from the pictures that were printed upon it, very similar to those upon the "pencilled china" that came into vogue about the same time. About 1761, mattresses stuffed with hair were offered for sale, but these did not, by any means, supplant in favour the feather bed and "sacking-bottom."

By the side, or at the foot of the bed, stood the bed-steps. At the other side, a small table with a candlestick was always to be found in a comfortable bedroom. In the early part of the century, a strip of carpet, called "a bedside carpet," to distinguish it from the carpet upon the bed (for the word carpet had not lost its first meaning), was placed beside the bed, but as the years advanced, rugs were more plentiful and a carpet frequently covered the entire floor. The bed was often covered with a spread, and the dressing-table with a "toilet" made by the ladies of the house.

The bedstead generally stood opposite the open fireplace, where the logs burned brightly upon brass andirons, guarded by a fender and supplied with shovel, tongs and bellows. A mahogany case-of-drawers standing upon its high cabriole legs and garnished with brass escutcheons and handles, and a small case-of-drawers, also bright with brass mounts, were conspicuous objects. Above the latter hung a dressing-glass. Perhaps there was also a large chest-upon-chest of drawers, or an old mahogany *kas*, or wardrobe, a "bureau table," a wash-stand, and almost always two or three small tables, upon one of which a set of tea-things stood ready for use. Sometimes were to be seen a "couch and squab" and a "lolling-chair" for further comfort, and very often a "scrutore," or large secretary.

The room was profusely ornamented with china. China vases and curious images decorated the chimney-piece and appeared on the top of the chest-upon-chest, or the tall case-of-drawers, provided the latter was not finished with the favourite scroll or "swan-neck" sweeps. Even then, in the centre from which they sprang, a small china vase, or other ornament was placed. A screen and a number of chairs completed the furniture. The latter might consist of a set of mahogany, including two arm-chairs, the seats matching the bed and window curtains, or they might be of cheaper wood with plain splat backs and rush seats, ordinary walnut frame and leather-bottom chairs, or of the cabriole leg with ball-and-claw foot and embowed back, the seat being of Turkey-work, worsted damask, or hair. Again, the chairs might have cane, or matted seats.

Next in importance to the bed in the up-stairs apartments were the high and low cases-of-drawers, popularly, but erroneously known to-day as the "high boy" and "low boy." These consisted of a series of drawers that stood on a frame composed of spindle-shaped legs connected by a straining-rail or stretcher, as shown in the example from the Museum of the New York Colonial Dames on page 57, or standing on the springing cabriole leg ending in the plain hoof, or the more ornate claw-and-ball foot. The former kind that stood on a frame of six legs generally had a square top; the latter variety frequently terminated in a scroll top. In addition to these pieces of furniture, there was the chest-of-drawers and the chest-upon-chest, of which an example in French walnut is here represented. This belonged to Mr. and Mrs. Augustus Van Horne (the latter a daughter of Frederick Van Cortlandt and Frances Jay), married

Chest-upon-chest, originally owned by Mr. and Mrs. Augustus Van Horne; now by Mr. and Mrs. Matthew Clarkson.

in 1765. It is now owned by Mr. and Mrs. Matthew Clarkson of New York, having descended to them through the Jay family. The brass escutcheons and handles on these pieces of furniture were important additions, and varied from simple drop-handles to patterns that were quite elaborate.

In the early part of the century, the chairs were of leather (one variety of which is shown on page 54), cane, and matted. The latter was popular about 1700, and was often of the kind represented on the same page. We also find in the early homes elbow chairs and easy chairs covered with red plush, or silk, or damask. About 1725, and onward, the walnut or mahogany chair with the claw-and-ball foot, was constantly used. This chair invariably came in sets, including two chairs with arms. The covers of the seats were of red leather, Turkey-work, silk, silk or worsted damask, the favourite colours being red, green and yellow. Types of these chairs appear on page 71.

In 1760, haircloth for chair-seating was imported. It continued long in fashion. Sometimes it was figured, and sometimes coloured. In 1765, Joseph Cox advertised " a variety of beautiful black horsehair for chair bottoms, such as are in the greatest vogue at home" (home being London); in 1771, "figured horsehair for chair bottoms;" and in 1772, "patterns of horsehair for chair bottoms."

Figured calico, chintz and copper-plate materials were used for furniture coverings and draperies towards the end of our period, especially in bedrooms.

With sets of chairs, the double chair, or settee, was often included. This was formed of two chair backs placed side by side and carved or perforated to match the single chairs. The "corner chair" that Joseph Cox made in 1773 was of the variety shown on page 104. This one is ornamented with a double back. The stuffed chair was often in use. Sometimes it was referred to as the " French " chair. The " burgair " chair, also in Cox's list, was an upholstered chair of special design.

The stuffed sofa gained in popularity. It was frequently draped in the most elaborate style with festoons caught in waves and swags, and fastened at regular intervals by a rosette. Sometimes it had a canopy carved in the Gothic or Chinese taste, and sometimes it was made to fit into an alcove and become a kind of couch-bed with curtains that were drawn into their symmetrical position by means of cords and tassels that connected with pullies. Chippendale was especially fond of fringe, cords and tassels for his sofas and beds, and for his ornate pieces recommends gold cords and tassels.

Before the middle of the century, the Windsor chair had become popular. An example is shown to the left of the bed, in the room on page 23. The Windsor chair was of various kinds and was painted in different colours. Many chair-makers devoted their energies solely to this kind of chair. The following advertisement of 1769 gives an idea of the industry :

"A large and neat Assortment of Windsor Chairs made in the best and neatest manner, and well-painted, viz., High-back'd, low back'd, and Sack backed Chairs and Settees or double seated fit for Piazza or Gardens, Children's Dining and low chairs, etc. To be sold by Jonathan Hampton in Chapel Street, New York, opposite Captain Andrew Law's."

The " scrutore," *escritoire*, or secretary, was found in both drawing-room and bedroom. It was often a combination bookcase and desk, the upper portion being enclosed by doors with panes of glass. Two specimens appear on pages 291 and 10. The former is said to have come from Holland, but it is similar in character to many that Chippendale included among his designs. This belonged originally to Ryck Suydam (1675–1741) supervisor of Flatbush, L. I. and is now owned by his descendant, Mrs. Henry Draper of New York. The second is also of mahogany and is of the "Gothic Style" of the day. This belonged to Thomas Barrow, and was brought by him to New York in 1764. It is now owned by a descendant. Another form of desk was a simple chest-of-drawers with a flap which, when let down, formed the table for writing.

In every home was a number of tables; in many cases, the rooms contained several devoted to different uses. The dining-table was of mahogany. The oak drawing-table had long been out of fashion, and the extension table with its additional leaves had not yet been introduced, so that when more room was desired, tables were added to the central one. These tables all had drop leaves supported upon a movable leg. A good specimen is illustrated on page 75. The straight leg ends in a ball-and-claw foot. This now belongs to Mrs. W. Sherwood Popham of New York. Nearly every house had its card-tables which were usually of walnut or mahogany, like the specimen shown on page 326, or of an older design with cabriole leg and ball-and-claw foot. The tea-table was of the utmost importance : it was of mahogany, painted, or japanned, or of walnut. Almost invariably, it revolved and could be made to tip as well as turn, and sometimes, when not in use, stood in the room in the position of the one shown on page 85. Of the three varieties of tea-tables, the one on page 312 was the older in design, as the "snake-foot" proclaims. The one on page 114 is more delicate in form and not only has the ball-and-claw foot but the acanthus carved upon the tripod legs. The third on page 85, is a more elaborate specimen and its large top is cut out of a solid piece of wood. The first belongs to the Barrow family ; the second, to Mrs. W. W. Shippen of New York ; the third, was originally owned by Col. and Mrs. John Cox of Bloomsbury, Trenton, but now belongs to Mrs. Edward Parke Custis Lewis of Hoboken, N. J.

A small mahogany stand, or table, was usually placed by the side of the bed, as shown on page 23. Previous to the advent of Heppelwhite, the sideboard in the dining-room was a long table with square ends. Chippendale, in his book of designs, does not give a single example of the sideboard as we know it to-day, nor is such a piece of furniture found among the plates of Darly, or Ince and Mayhew. The "sideboard table" that Chippendale recommends often has its framework richly carved in Gothic, or Chinese style. Therefore, when we are told that so many tables were in the dining-room, we are not wrong if we call one of them "a sideboard table."

The tea-table was present in every room. The number of articles used in the service of tea was considerable. Mahogany tea-boards (little tables), tea-chests, cannisters, lamps, kettles and nests of kettles, kettles with lamps, tea-tongs, sugar-cleavers, sugar-tongs, spoons, urns, tea-trays, etc., etc., of all varieties appear again and again. The tea-kettle stand was also important, and the tea-tray was of many kinds and sizes. It was frequently of mahogany with a carved rim in the Chinese or Gothic taste ; but hardly less popular was the tray that was painted and ja-panned. We give two of these : the one on page 321 dates from the beginning of our period ; the second, on page 100, from towards the end. Like the painted and japanned tea-table, it was always a favourite. The former is said to have been brought to America in 1686. It is now in the Museum of the Colonial Dames at Van Cortlandt. The picture upon it is a landscape. The second, is a more beautiful example and is decorated with a charming oil painting after Joseph Vernet. It is now in the Museum for the Art of Decoration at the Cooper Union, New York. Tea-trays and waiters "of the newest fashion with landscapes" were still coming in in 1781.

Japanned-ware was popular throughout the Eighteenth Century. It was not only used for tea-trays, tea-kitchens, tea-tables, cannisters, sugar-boxes, and knife-cases, but for dressing-tables, clock-cases, chairs and every other style of furniture. As early as 1734, we find "eight-day clocks with japan cases" offered for sale by John Bell, and, as late as 1771, Stephen Gueubel of Wall Street announced to the "nobility and gentry" that he had "just arrived in this city" and had for sale "a quantity of beautiful furniture elegantly painted and varnished in the *Japan taste*" and had "some complete toilets." He also undertook to "paint coaches and chairs in the same manner."

In 1772, Jane Wilson in the Fly Market offered a "great variety of beautiful japanned goods with cream

Walnut chair and mahogany tea-table, owned by Mrs. W. W. Shippen.
See page 112.

coloured grounds and other colours of the newest taste." Her wares included tea-tables, tea-chests with cannisters, tea-trays, bread-baskets and inkstands ; and she also had " some white japanned clock-faces, which have the appearance of enamelled watch-plates." Although there were many watch and clock-makers in New York, the ships constantly brought clocks and clock-cases to New York. The tall clock with its brass dial, frequently embellished with the changes of the moon, and occasionally equipped with machinery for telling the tides, was the favourite. Bracket and pedestal clocks were also in use ; and many clocks were furnished with musical chimes.

Nearly every household owned a tall clock, and in many houses the enormous clothes-press known as the *Kas* was frequently found. This, of course, was of Dutch origin and corresponded to the more modern wardrobe. Another piece of furniture that the English found when they arrived was the cabinet in which the citizens of New Amsterdam kept their choicest china and other curios.

"Thomas Ash, Windsor chair-maker." (1774.)

PART III
TABLE FURNISHINGS

PART III

TABLE FURNISHINGS

I

CHINA, USEFUL AND ORNAMENTAL

OCCASIONALLY, one hears it said that there was little or no china in New York before the Revolution ; but whoever will pause to think for a moment will know that this could not be true. The Dutch, as is well known, were among the very first collectors of china in Europe. It is not likely that the Dutch ships constantly arriving in New Amsterdam should fail to import wares of this nature. Indeed, china and porcelain were to be found in Dutch homes on this side of the Atlantic, in great quantity, before the English satirists attacked the china-mania.

The home of Cornelis Steenwyck, who died in 1686, was profusely decorated with china. In one room alone—the Great Chamber—there were no less than " nineteen porcelain dishes," besides two flowered earthen pots. Margarita Van Varick was another person who possessed a vast amount of china. She had three East India cups and three East India dishes, three " cheenie pots," " one cheenie cup bound with silver," " two glassen cases with thirty-nine pieces of small chinaware," and eleven " Indian babyes."

Besides this, there were 126 pieces of chinaware, consisting of cups, saucers, tea-cups, dishes, basons, jugs, flower-pots, toys and images.

Mr. Jacob De Lange, who died in 1685, had a magnificent collection that would be priceless to-day. It included 164 separate pieces.

Francis Rombouts (1692), had one Holland cupboard furnished with porcelain and earthenware, worth £15; and another, valued at £5-13-0.

Cornelis Jacobs (1700), owned a china lacquered bowl and a parcel of chinaware and earthenware, twelve new plates and nine earthen dishes. Abraham

Group of ornamental earthenware, owned by Mrs. F. H. Bosworth.
See page 127.

DeLanoy (1702), had 120 dishes, cups and saucers; Colonel William Smith of St. Georges (1705), had chinaware worth £5; Joseph Nunes (1705), had "one small Delph plate", Joseph Bueno (1709), had an earthen woman and a dog; seven china cups; twelve cups and saucers; and five images in glasses.

Table Furnishings

Capt. Giles Shelly (1718) owned much china, including a punch-bowl, "six chaney lions," eleven images, three "chaney basons," a red tea-pot, a sugar-box, an image and much earthenware; George Duncan (1724) possessed much earthenware and china, among which were seven images and a box with images; Governor Burnet's china and glass amounted to £130–16–0; and Governor Montgomerie had a set of china valued at £75.

The people of this period valued their china highly. They kept it in cabinets and cases with glass doors, on shelves, and in racks made especially for it, besides decorating with it mantel-pieces and the tops of cupboards, cases, presses and chests-of-drawers. Much of the china was purely ornamental, such as birds, animals, figures, and images. Specimens of the china images of the period are shown on page 361. These horses are white with trappings of the brightest colours. They are owned by Mrs. F. H. Bosworth.

Much of the china of the day, having come from the Orient, was exceedingly handsome, and was disposed of in special bequests. For instance, in 1684, Judith Stuyvesant left to her son, Nicholas, all her china "except the three great pots." These she left "To my cousin, Nicholas Bayard" and "My black cabinet of ebben wood with the foot or frame belonging to it, together with the three great china pots before reserved."

There is no reason why these three great pots should not have been similar to those shown on page 77, which have been for many years in the Beekman family. This covered jar and two beakers are of the famous old Hizen ware, and were probably made about two hundred years ago. It may be said here that in the province of Hizen were two ports, one of which, Nagasaki, was the seat of the Dutch trade after 1641, and the other, Imari, the port from which most of the china was exported. One peculiarity of Hizen ware is that it somewhat resembles Chinese art. From Imari were sent two kinds of china: one, decorated with red, blue and gold; the other, merely with blue. The style of decoration consists of medallions representing landscapes or figures framed in branches of chrysanthemum, peony, fir, or bamboo. The jars on page 77 are of the red and blue variety. They were in the home of the Beekmans at " Rural Cove," New York and are still owned by the family.

A specimen of the ordinary Dutch cabinet filled with china, brass and copper-ware of the period, showing exactly what might have been found in the simplest home of New Amsterdam, is, with its contents, shown on page 356. People of such wealth as Cornelis Steenwyck, Jacob De Lange, and Margarita Van Varick owned much handsomer cases and cabinets for the display of their curios; but such a cabinet as the above was not beyond the reach of any one.

From the arrival of the English down to the Revolution, china was imported in increasingly large quantities from year to year. Among the largest importers were James Gilliland in Wall Street and later in Canon's Dock; John J. Roosevelt, Maiden Lane; George Bell, Bayard Street; and Henry Wilmot, Hanover Square. Every now and then, they advertised large assortments of china and earthenware of the "newest fashion," and very frequently they described their goods.

It must be remembered that the various English potteries were in their full glory. The Elers were working near Burslem, producing a red ware similar to Japanese pottery, salt-glaze and black ware ; at Burslem, Aaron Wood, Thomas Whieldon and John Mitchell were turning out yellowish white and cream-coloured salt-glaze, tortoiseshell, cauliflower and melon ware, and agate ware, and Wedgwood was improving every variety in partnership with Whieldon and later with Bentley. Liverpool, Worcester, Leeds, Yorkshire, Chelsea, Plymouth, Bow, Lowestoft, Swansea, and other noted English potteries were at the period of their greatest activity, so that when we read such a simple announcement in 1757 as that James McEvers has for sale "china ware by the chest, newest fashion," or that Gregg and Cunningham at their store in Queen Street have "a few hogsheads of earthenware, containing punch-bowls and plates, crates containing cups, saucers and tea-pots; also a parcel of common earthenware" (1756), we can tell very well what kind of articles went into New York homes. The following advertisement of 1757 is a little more detailed :

"To be sold by Edward Nicoll on the New Dock crates of common yellow ware, both cups and dishes; crates of white stone cups and saucers; crates of blue and white ditto; crates of white ware; crates of blue and white; crates of black; crates of tortoise shell and crates of red, all well sorted; crates of pocket bottles, boxes of glass, consisting of wine glass; salts, sugar dishes, cream pots and tumblers; tierces and hogsheads

White enamelled and salt glaze earthenware, owned by Mrs. F. H. Bosworth.

See page 125.

of Delft ware, consisting of punch-bowls, dishes, tea-cups and saucers; with a large and good assortment of earthenware and glass; and a parcel of fine mosaic dishes and plates by retail."

Nothing throughout our period was more popular than cream-coloured earthenware glazed with salt, upon which Wedgwood experimented until he produced the famous cream between 1761 and 1765. It attracted the attention of Queen Charlotte and thenceforth became known as Queen's Ware. It constantly appears in the New York advertisements after 1765.

Cream-coloured ware from Leeds, similar to the Staffordshire Queen's Ware, was also popular. It occurred most frequently in the basket, or wicker, pattern and was exceedingly light in weight. A choice group of this kind of ware appears on page 124. It belongs to Mrs. F. H. Bosworth. Here we find basket and perforated plates, a fruit-dish with a cover imitating various fruits, and a sauce-boat in the shape of a melon resting on a leaf, with a stem gracefully twisted to form a handle.

Lowestoft ware was made as early as 1752. Chinese patterns and floral patterns (particularly the pink rose), were the designs in most universal use. Very frequently, fine tea-sets and dessert services were decorated to order with coats-of-arms, crests, or cyphers, accompanied by a floral or scroll border. This ware was also imported into New York. A tea-set that was given to Gen. and Mrs. Hezekiah Barnes, in 1780, on the occasion of their wedding, appears on page 126. It might, however, be of earlier date. This set is now in the Museum of the Colonial Dames at Van Cortlandt, New York.

A good idea of the china that was used in 1762 may be obtained by referring to the stock of Keeting and Morris, who had removed from Beekman's Slip to the New Dock and announced " a compleat assort-

Lowestoft china in the Museum of the New York Colonial Dames. See page 125.

ment of the most fashionable kinds of Glass and Stone-Ware." This included " table plates and dishes both of the oval and round shape, black tea-pots, mugs and bowls of all sizes, tortoise, table plates and dishes of the newest patterns, green and tortoise tea-pots, milk pots, bowls, cups and saucers, Venice flower vases and horns, glass quart, pint, and half pint decanters, wine glasses, enamelled stone tea-pots, mugs, bowls and tea-cups, and saucers of all sizes and of the newest patterns, with a great variety of plain white ware."

There was no less interest in quaint figures of animals, birds, images and curious objects than there was in the days of the Dutch. Ornamental china was made in great quantities, particularly at Chelsea, Plymouth and Bow. Busts also grew in popularity.

These were generally of earthenware brightly painted. Shakespeare, Milton, George II., George III., Wolfe, Chatham, and all the popular heroes, poets and actors of the day could be had. Other ornaments for chimney-pieces, tops of bookcases, chests-of-drawers, shelves and cabinets, included brightly painted birds, cats, dogs, lambs, shepherds and shepherdesses, mythological figures, figures of Britannia seated on a lion, Minerva with shield, owl, and books, Neptune with trident on a base of shells and rock-work, lovers, pastoral figures, allegorical figures, such as the Seasons, etc., etc. A typical group of such ware appears on page 120. This belongs to Mrs. F. H. Bosworth.

A few citations of importations will show how popular was this form of decoration; for example: "some beautiful ornamental chimney china" 1766; "white stone-ware, including complete tea-table toys for children, with a great collection of different kinds of birds, beasts, etc., in stoneware, very ornamental for mantle-pieces, chests-of-drawers, etc.," 1767; "one set of image china," 1768; "the greatest variety of ornamental china, consisting of groups, setts of figures, pairs and jars just opened," 1770; and "birds and baskets of flowers for the tops of bookcases," 1775.

Oriental ware never declines in popularity. Dinner services, tea-pots, cups and saucers, vases, etc., come from Canton and Nankin as in modern days. A few dishes, with a salad-bowl and soup tureen that belonged to William Denning about 1765, are shown on page 93. They show the kind of Oriental china that was in common use in the best New York houses.

A tea-table set of Nankin china was mentioned among the private sales in 1773.

The taste for Eastern art was not shared by every one, however, for in a long fable in 1754, we read the following description of a tea-pot that was evidently the fashion :

> " A tawdry Tea Pot *à la mode*
> Where Art her utmost skill bestow'd,
> Was much esteem'd for being old,
> And on its sides with Red and Gold
> Strange Beasts were drawn in taste Chinese,
> And frightful Fish and hump-backed Trees.
> High in an elegant beaufet
> This pompous Utensil was set.
> And near it on a Marble Slab
> Forsaken by some careless Drab
> A veteran Scrubbing Brush was plac'd
> And the rich Furniture disgrac'd."

Some of the families that inherited old china always kept it jealously. A few examples still survive. They have conquered every change of fashion. On page 129 is a pair of " Mandarin vases," originally owned by William de Peyster, who died in 1784. He also owned the richly decorated Oriental bowl that appears on the same plate. These three pieces were buried for safety, during the Revolution. Between the vases is a plate that belonged to Margaret Livingston in 1758.

In 1767, we note that Breese and Hoffman, of Wall Street, had imported " India china, enamelled and blue and white bowls, caudle cups, blue and white cups and saucers, with small sets of service china, and Nankin china mugs." Among the lists of importations from 1750 to 1775, are found English Delft, blue and white earthenware, japanned, gilded, green, agate, tortoiseshell, Tunbridge, Porto-bello, cream-coloured, brown edged sprig, enamelled burnt china, quilted china, cauliflower and melon, black, pencilled, Dresden, Staffordshire and flint

Vases, bowl and plate originally owned by William de Peyster, and now by the family of the late James de Peyster.   See page 128.

ware.   Pine-apple and " colly flower coffee pots," white tortoise mugs and jugs, black ware and agate and melloned ware were advertised in 1765–'6 ; while white and enamelled tea-table sets, white and burnt china bowls, blue and white enamelled china, blue and white landscape china, enamelled white and gilt landscape, nankin, brown edged sprig and duck breakfast cups and saucers, black and white ribbed and engraved china, burnt china, and white, quilted and plain china were imported in 1767; burnt china jars and beakers, fruit-baskets, sauce-boats and "pickel" leaves in 1772; "burnt china, quilted china, pencil'd china, blue and white Queen's ware, Delph, and stone enamelled black," in 1773; blue and white, blue and gold, purple and gold and enamelled and burnt, in 1774; "elegant sets of Dresden tea table china and ornamental jars and figures decorated and enriched in the highest taste," in 1775; and "very handsome red china tea-pots, Wedgwood's," in 1778.

In view of these importations, it may be interesting to define a few of the varieties mentioned. The tortoiseshell ware was covered with a mottled glaze,

Group of Wedgwood, owned by Mrs. F. H. Bosworth. See page 132.

brown, purple or green. Frequently, wine cups and drinking-glasses were made of this. A specimen cup with the head of Bacchus appears on page 120.

Agate was variegated ware, imitating agate or marble, and was made by mixing different clays together. Cauliflower ware imitated that vegetable in form and colour, and was especially attractive to potters of the day who prided themselves on their green glaze and cream-coloured body. Pickle-leaves were dishes in imitation of the leaf ; the pineapple was imitated, for jugs and tea-pots ; the lettuce was used frequently for bowls and jugs ; and the favourite melon ware included melons and other fruits. The Portobello ware was made by Astbury in 1727 after the expedition of Admiral Vernon, who took Portobello.

There was also a great demand for the decorated painted and enamelled china. The china was ornamented with portraits of George II., Queen Charlotte, William Pitt, George III. and Shakespeare, and pictures of the Four Seasons, Freemasons' Arms, Masonic Emblems, Milkmaid and other pastoral scenes after Watteau, Milkmaids and May Dance after Gainsborough, Garden Scenes, Tea Parties, Landscapes with Ruins and River Scenes, Chinese Landscapes and Figures, Fishing and Garden Parties, Haymakers, Architectural Ruins after Panini, and pictures after Angelica Kauffman, Cipriani, Cosway and Bartolozzi. Much of this came from Worcester, Liverpool and Battersea.

In all probability, this ware was the "pencilled" china so frequently mentioned among the late importations. Quilted china was done somewhat after the style of the pineapple and cauliflower ware, and much of it was made at St. Cloud in France.

The most famous of the many famous English potters, however, was Josiah Wedgwood, who made every kind of ware that we have mentioned and

adapted it to every article, including snuff-boxes, candlesticks, inkstands and the handles of knives and
forks. The first ware that brought fame to Wedgwood was the "cream coloured," which, as we have
seen, became the Queen's Ware. Then he made a
kind of red ware after the style of the Elers ; and,
in 1766, the black ware, which he called basaltes, or
black Egyptian. In 1773, he made a fine white terra
cotta of great beauty and delicacy fit for cameos, portraits and bas-reliefs, and in 1776 the famous jasper
ware that could be made of any tint,—such as light
and dark blue, pale buff, salmon-pink or sage-green.
An interesting group of Wedgwood specimens appears on page 130, owned by Mrs. F. H. Bosworth,
of New York. There are upon this illustration several pieces of black basalt, jasper ware of pale blue,
lapis lazuli, sage-green and buff enriched with cameos
and festoons, and a white vase. In the centre is a
tea-pot of black basalt.

Although the New York families were constantly
buying china of the latest fashions, they took great
care of the pieces that had long been in their homes,
as is shown by the number of men who made a business of repairing. One of these, Jacob Da Costa in
Batteau Street, advertised in 1769, that he "mends
broken china with rivets and cement, mends all sorts
of marble or china furniture, such as is used for
ornamenting chimney-pieces, chests-of-drawers, etc.,
mends the necks of decanters that have been broken,
hoops glass and china mugs that have been cracked
and mends ladies' fans."

II

PLATE, TANKARDS, PUNCH BOWLS AND CANDLESTICKS

WROUGHT silver was always highly prized. From the first settlement of this country, every prosperous householder possessed pieces of plate. In New York, before 1700, examples occur in numerous inventories of English, Dutch and French homes. Thomas Eaton in 1668, bequeathed to Mrs. Abigail Nicolls, "my silver boat, my silver meat fork, and a silver spoon." George Cook's silver, in 1679, was worth £40. John Sharpe, in 1681, owned 730 oz. of silver plate valued at £219.

At that date, wrought silver was worth six shillings and eightpence an ounce. It may be mentioned here that its value averaged about seven shillings an ounce for the next two hundred years. Col. Lewis Morris (1691), had 900 oz. of silver plate, which at 6 sh. 9d. per oz. came to £303–15.0. Five years later, 185 oz. belonging to Margarita Van Varick was valued at 7 sh. 9d per oz. Besides this 185 oz., which was probably in the form of cups, beakers, salvers, etc., she had a lot of miscellaneous articles in silver.

These comprised two pairs of scissors, two brushes lined with silver, a spice-box, an egg-dish, a thimble, a wrought East India box, a small knife and fork, three wrought East Indian cups, two wrought East Indian dishes, two knives, five wrought East Indian boxes, a tumbler marked R. V., a fork with studded handle, a wrought East Indian trunk, a salt-cellar, a china cup bound with silver, and eighty-three play-things, or toys. All these items were separately specified as silver. Some of the individual prices of plate of this period may be of interest. In 1690, it is expressly stated that six large and three small spoons together with six forks, belonging to Madame Blanche Sauzeau, cost £10. In 1686, a silver beaker belong-ing to Derick Clausen was appraised at £3; and the 295 oz. belonging to Sarah Jacobs were valued at seven shillings per ounce.

Asser Levy, a butcher in 1683, was evidently fond of plate. His pieces comprise twenty-two silver spoons, one fork, three goblets, one tumbler, one tankard, one mustard pot, one cup with two ears, five small cups, one ditto, one gob-let, two salt-cellars, one cup, one spice-box, a cornelia tree cup with silver and two ditto dishes, weighing in all 10 lbs. and valued at £48. His total estate was £553–15–0.

Silver tankard, owned by Frederic J. de Peyster, Esq. See page 137.

William Cox (1689), owned a case of silver hafted knives, silver tankard, cup, plate, sugar-box and spoon, salt-cellar, two porringers, tumbler and twelve spoons.

It is thus abundantly evident that, at the opening of our period, the chests, kasses and cupboards of the

New York traders were well supplied with plate. But before going further in our examination of the Eighteenth Century silver, it will be well to recapitulate those articles most commonly found already. These are the dram cup, the caudle cup, the salt, the beaker, the salver, the tumbler, the goblet, the tankard, and the porringer. In addition to these, there were boxes for spices, pepper and sugar, besides knives, spoons, forks and candlesticks. It must be remembered, however, that even in 1700 the fork was not yet universally used. The voider was a dish or tray into which crumbs and fragments of food were swept from the table after a meal. The "voyder knife" used for this purpose is frequently mentioned in the inventories. The voider soon came into general use: families that could not afford one of silver, had one painted, or japanned, or made of mahogany.

The "salt" still preserved its massive Mediæval character in many cases, though the low circular, or octagonal, form was rapidly driving it out. Twenty ounces was not an excessive weight for one of the high chased and carved "salts" used here in 1700.

A great water-pot with its cover, belonging to James Laty, in 1692, was, perhaps, one of those fine ewers employed for pouring water over the hands after every course at meals in an age when forks were not in general use. They were accompanied by basins, similarly ornamented. The description, however, would rather fit the "tankard" that came into general use during the Seventeenth Century. The word was originally applied to a receptacle for water,—tub, bucket, or jug—and gradually restricted to mean a

silver or pewter mug with handle or cover. From
the accession of Charles II. to that of George I. this

article was usually
plain in form and de-
sign, with flat hinged
lids and heavy han-
dles, the latter some-
times terminating in
a whistle. The later
"Queen Anne" tank-
ards, however, had a
swelling drum and
domed lid, some-
times ending in a
knob. Their orna-
mentation principal-
ly consisted of the
arms and monograms
of the owners. Some-

Silver candlesticks (1762–'3), originally
owned by Samuel and Judith Ver Planck.
See page 143.

times silver coins were embedded in the lids of these
tankards. Thus, in 1733:

"Stole at Flatbush on Long Island One Silver Tank-
ard, a piece of Money in the Led of King Charles II. and the
Led all ingraved, a Coat of Arms before (in it a Man on a
Waggon with two Horses) marked in the handle L P A. One
Silver Tankard plain with a piece of Money in the Led,
mark'd on the Handle A P or A L. One Cup with two twisted
Ears chas'd with Skutchens mark'd L P A. One Tumbler
mark'd L P A. One Dutch Beker weighs about 28 Ounces
Engrav'd all round mark'd L P A. All the above was made
by Jacob Boele, Stamp'd I. B. One large Cup with two cast
Ears, with Heads upon them and a Coat of arms Engrav'd
thereon. One Cup with two Ears, a small Hole in the bottom.
Whoever can inform Peter Lefferts of Flatbus   Long Island,

or Abraham Lefferts in New York, so that it may be had again, shall have Fifteen Pounds Reward and no Questions asked."

A very fine authentic example of this style is owned by Frederic J. de Peyster, Esq. and appears on page 134. Another that belonged to William Beekman is represented on page 179. A later form of tankard appears on page 156. The hall-mark shows that this was made in 1749–'50. It belonged to James Alexander and is now owned by Mrs. Edward Parke Custis Lewis of Hoboken, N. J. Another early Eighteenth century tankard appears on page 153. A fifth is shown on page 371 ; it belonged to Maria Crooke who gave it to her daughter, Catharine Elmendorph in 1768 when she was married to Rutgers Bleecker of Albany. The tankard is engraved with the Crooke arms.

A sixth tankard, shown on page 138, is marked on the handle $_{R.S.}^{R.}$, the initials standing for Richard and Sarah (Bogert) Ray whose pictures appear on pages 195 and 202. This piece of silver was bequeathed to their son Cornelius Ray (1755–1827), whose initials with crest (Ray) are engraved on the front of the tankard. The large mug has the same initials, and the small mug contains the crest, but not the markings on the handle. The soup-ladle, which is an unusually fine specimen, is also marked with the Ray initials. These are now owned by a descendant, Mrs. Natalie E. Baylies of New York.

The slop-bowl with cover, in the same illustration, belonged to Elizabeth Elmendorph who married Cornelius Ray and is now owned by their granddaughter, Mrs. Natalie E. Baylies. The large silver salver hanging above these smaller articles has the date letter of 1784–'5 and is engraved with the arms of the English family of Sands. It was given by Comfort Sands to his daughter, Cornelia, in 1797 when she was married to Nathaniel Prime. She gave it to Rufus Prime and it passed from Temple Prime to Mrs. Natalie E. Baylies.

Silver belonging to the Sands and Ray families ; now owned by Mrs. Natalie E. Baylies. See page 137.

The two silver mugs standing on the tea-table (page 312) are excellent specimens of the period. They were owned by Thomas Barrow and brought by him to New York. They are dated H, the letter for the year 1763–'4, and are ornamented with scroll-work, flowers and pavilions in the Chinese taste.

Tumblers are often found. These received their

name from the fact that no matter how you laid them down, they were so balanced as always to assume an upright position, swaying from side to side till they came to rest on their own base. These round-bottomed acrobatic cups, or tumblers, were sometimes called bowls in the inventories, and were of different sizes;—the larger for beer and the smaller for wine.

Caudle-cups, which frequently occur, were also known as posset-cups or posnets. At the present time they would probably be designated loving-cups. They had two handles and a cover, and sometimes stood on a tray. They were wider at the base than at the top and were used for drinking posset, which was a concoction of milk curdled with wine, and other ingredients. Bowls, also with covers and handles, but wider in the mouth than the caudle-cup, were called porringers. Instead of being circular in form, they sometimes had eight or twelve sides. The Queen Anne fluted porringers were often used as beer cups. Earlier specimens were ornamented with acanthus and other leaves and floral devices in *repoussé* work. As time went on, the porringer became taller in proportion to its diameter and the handles more slender and graceful. Another important piece of plate was the punch-bowl. This occurs in innumerable inventories during the Seventeenth and Eighteenth Centuries from Salem to Charleston.

The handsome silver punch-bowl on page 140 now belonging to Frederic J. de Peyster, Esq., is of English make as its hall-marks show. It dates from the year 1704, and is almost identical with one in

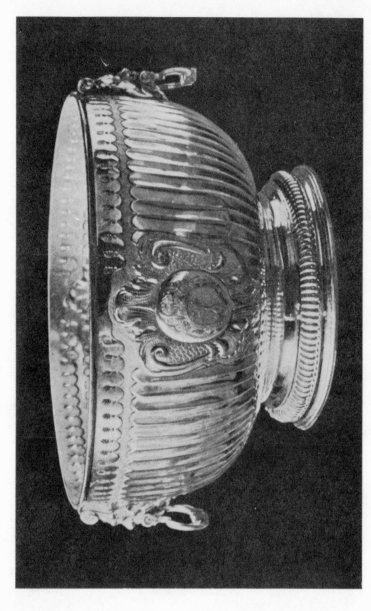

Silver punch-bowl (1704) owned by Frederic J. de Peyster, Esq.

possession of the Vintners Company, London, which is of the year 1702. The fluted bowl, the large rings depending from the lions' heads, and the gadrooned base are characteristics of this period.

This kind of punch-bowl was usually called a Monteith, from a scalloped or battlemented rim that was placed on the top of the bowl for the purpose of carrying the glasses. The name was given to it on account of its association with a gentleman of fashion who was noted for wearing a scalloped coat. The glasses were arranged in the scalloped rim with their bases outward. The bowl was brought in empty, for every gentleman took pride in mixing punch. The various ingredients and the ladle were brought in with the bowl. When the bowl was placed on the table, the glasses were first lifted out of the rim and then the rim was removed. Punch ladles were of silver, or horn tipped with silver. One, of silver with a twisted ebony handle, appears on page 388. Punch-strainers were also used.

Ewers and basins became plentiful before 1700, the absence of forks, as has been said, rendering them very necessary at meals. The great number of napkins in every home of wealth is thus accounted for also. The salvers that accompanied the helmet-shaped ewers were usually quite plain. The other salvers, about 1700, were plain circular dishes with engraved ornamentation. The engraving as a decoration had taken the place of the *repoussé* work of the earlier styles, some of which are very beautifully wrought. A magnificent specimen is shown on page 394. The De Peyster arms are stamped in the centre.

The "Queen Anne" salvers have their edges both chased and shaped, and they stand on three and sometimes four small feet. The plainer ones are often gadrooned around the edges.

The succeeding style of salver had a beaded edge, and instead of being circular, or shaped, was a plain oval tray with a handle at each end. One of these appears on page 156 with one of older date above it. The lower one was given by Gen. Washington to Eleanor Custis. The hall-mark shows that it was made in England in 1797. The Lewis arms are engraved upon it. It is interesting as showing how long this style lasted,—at least, till the end of the century. The small salver, above it of very handsome design, has the hall-mark 1743. It belongs to Miss Garnett of Hoboken, N. J. On the same plate are shown two coffee-pots, one of which belonged to James Alexander (see page 76), a tea-pot with hall-mark of 1749-'50; a tankard (1749-'50) and a sugar-dredger.

Candelabra, candlesticks and sconces of silver were found in fashionable homes very early in the history of New York. The big "standing candlestick" often had two or three arms or branches. The candlesticks in the form of fluted columns were the favourite form in the reign of Charles II. They lasted for many years. The bases were generally square, but sometimes octagonal. At a certain height above the base, these candlesticks had a projection that served as a knob by which they could be conveniently held or carried. This simple form remained in fashion through the reigns of William and Mary, and Anne, but the fluted columns changed to baluster stems with square bases having the corners sometimes cut off, and sometimes set back and rounded.

During the reign of George I. the florid ornamentation and twisted work of the Regency and early Louis Quinze style came into vogue, especially the designs of Meissonier. Good examples are the candlesticks on page 136 and the very beautiful tea-kettle and stand on page 36, both of which belonged to the Ver Planck family. The candlesticks are part of a set of six originally owned by Samuel and Judith Crommelin Ver Planck. The hall-mark shows that they were made in 1762. These are now owned by Mr. William E. Ver Planck of New York. The tea-kettle on page 36 has the same hall-mark, and is now owned by Mrs. Louis Fitzgerald, of New York.

At the beginning of the reign of George III., the fashionable pattern for the candlestick was the Corinthian column, and this was the first style that invariably had a removable socket-pan. Fine examples are shown on page 150. These bear the hall-marks of 1766 and belonged to the Waltons (see pages 19 and 69). Four candlesticks of the same period, owned by Frederic J. de Peyster, Esq., appear on page 270.

Every home that had any pretensions to wealth or fashion was supplied with silver candlesticks for at least one room. Glass was also very fashionable for sconces. In 1729, Governor Burnet owned twelve silver candlesticks weighing $171\frac{1}{2}$ oz., two branches for three lights and two large glass sconces with glass arms. (See page 63.)

Like the china, the plate was often kept in cupboards made for its display. Among the possessions of George Duncan (1724), who owned 258 oz. of silver, we find a plate case with glass doors valued at £3–5–0. These cupboards did not afford much protection against theft, and rendered the burglar's task easy. We find many advertisements of stolen plate, with rewards for its recovery. In most cases it bears the arms and almost invariably the initials of the owner. Several contemporary engravers found plenty of employment in New York. In 1755, Henry Dawkins, engraver, lives opposite the Merchants' Coffee House. In 1763, "Joseph Simons seal-cutter and engraver from Berlin, cuts all sorts of coats-of-arms, cyphers etc. in stone, steel, silver, or any other metal, also engraves coats-of-arms, crests and cyphers on plate &c."

" For Bristol, the brigantine *Phila*, freight and passage, Cruger's wharf." (1773.)

III

BESIDES the plate imported from France, England and Holland, a considerable quantity was manufactured here. On the revocation of the Edict of Nantes, many of the best workers in the precious metals left France and settled in Holland, Germany and England. Not a few crossed the Atlantic. The names of the silversmiths who were freemen of New York from the close of the Seventeenth Century till the Revolution were as follows: Everardus Bogardus, Ahasuerus Kendrick, Cornelis Kiersteade and Benjamin Wyncoope (1698); Richard Overin and Jacob Vanderspiegel (1701); Benjamin Kip (1702); Bartolo Schaats (1708); Cornelis Cornelison (1712); Coenraet Ten Eyck (1716); Peter Vergereau (1721); Samuel Broadhurst (1725); John Hastier (1726); Cornelius Wynkoop (1727); Stephen Bourdet (1730); John Brevoort (1742); Silvester Morris (1759); John Burt Lyng and John Heath (1761); Joshua Slydell and William Grigg (1765); Walter Thomas (1769); and John Rominie (1770).

It will be noticed that some of the above names are unmistakably Huguenot, while others are English and Dutch. Besides these freemen, other silversmiths kept shops in New York and advertised in the papers. In 1767, Cary Dunn was in New Dutch Church

Street. Joseph Pinto of Bayard Street was a silversmith who kept his wares prominently before the public. In 1759 he announced :

"Very neat chased silver tea pots, sugar pots, mugs chased and plain, milk pots, coffee pots, pepper castors, salts with shovels and glasses to them, fluted and chased children's whistles, double and single jointed tea tongs, tea spoons, punch strainers and ladles."

He also sold "crystal and paste shoe, knee, stock and girdle buckles" and in 1761 he offered :

"Very fine silver chased turene, dish and spoon; chased and plain stands, full finished; chased candlesticks, coffee and tea pots, sugar dishes, slop bowls, and sauce boats, chased and plain pint and half pint mugs, salvers of different sizes, and milk pots, salts and pepper castors and narrow spoons, cases with silver-handled knives and forks, silver watches, silver and plated spurs, chased and plain whistles, gold-headed canes, locket buttons set in gold, shoe, knee and girdle buckles."

In the same year, he had a few additional articles, including silver chased coffee-pots, tea-pots and sugar-dishes, punch-strainers and ladles, and a "great variety of open-worked stone, knee and girdle buckles, gold and silver brooches set with garnets, plain gold do., crystal buttons set in gold and a variety of other things." Another silversmith who was anxious to serve the public was Benjamin Halsted. On one occasion at least, he does not seem to have given entire satisfaction, judging from the following announcement in 1764 :

"A premonition to those gentlemen that may hereafter have an occasion to employ a silversmith to beware of that villain Benjamin Halsted; lest they be bit by him as I have been. Andrew Bowne."

Table Furnishings

A few representative lists of plate actually owned by families about the middle of the century will show that the New York merchant's table was as well supplied as his brother's in England. Rip Van Dam, (see page 86) possessed a good deal of valuable silver

Urn, coffee-pot, spoons, *étui case* and snuff-box owned by the Lynson, Rutgers and Ludlow families. See page 152.

among which may be mentioned three tankards relatively worth $50.00, $35.00 and $60.00; a chafing-dish, $35.00; two candlesticks, snuffers and stand, $80.00; three castors, $30.00; two salvers worth $40.00 and $18.00; mug, salt-cellar and pepper-box, $20.00; two dozen spoons, $18.00; a pot, $14.00; and tea-spoons and table spoons, $25.00. The de Peyster plate, in 1760, consisted of four tankards, two decanters, two

147

dishes, three plates, seven salvers, two large salvers, two small salvers, two cups and covers, two chafing-dishes, six porringers, four sauce-boats, two punch-bowls, three mugs, four sugar-dishes, a coffee-pot and tea-pot, seven salts and shovels, one saucepan, four pairs of snuffers and stand, a mustard-pot, a bread-basket, a dram-bottle, a tobacco-dish, nine castors, six candlesticks, one waiter, twenty-three forks, three soup-spoons, two punch-ladles, ten tablespoons, ten tea-spoons, two sugar-tongs — all weighing 1272 ounces,—valued at from $1,500 to $2,000.

Some specimens of silver that were long in the de Peyster family appear on pages 140 and 394. Others, including an urn, coffee-pot, salvers, a tea-caddy, a mug, a strainer, ladles, candlesticks and grape-vine spoons appear on page 153. These are owned by the family of the late James de Peyster of New York.

The silver in the Walton house (described on page 69), might have indeed been described as "massy plate," amounting as it did to $340\frac{3}{4}$ ounces. It consisted of two pairs of silver candlesticks, $81\frac{1}{4}$ ounces; one silver snuffers stand, $11\frac{1}{4}$; one large silver waiter, 32; two small silver waiters, $15\frac{1}{2}$; two pint mugs, $21\frac{3}{4}$; two pint bowls, $12\frac{1}{2}$; two sauce-boats, 29; four salts and four shovels, $12\frac{1}{2}$; twenty tea-spoons; one sugar-tongs, 1; one small chafing-dish, 1; one punch-ladle, $\frac{1}{2}$; one wine-cock, 5; two table-spoons, $4\frac{1}{2}$; one tankard, $31\frac{3}{4}$; one punch-strainer, $1\frac{1}{4}$; one coffee-pot, 28; one large soup-spoon, 8; one large tankard, 44; and two large cases of knives, forks, and spoons. Two of the above candlesticks appear on page 150.

We have seen that during the Eighteenth Cen-

tury, it was not an exceptional case for a wealthy
home to contain plate weighing 1000 oz. and sometimes considerably more. It will be interesting to
see of what a typical collection of this kind, though
only of about half the above amount, consisted.

	oz.	dwts.
1 silver tea-kettle, lamp and stand	107	14
1 waiter	82	10
1 saucepan	23	15
1 chafing-dish	23	14
1 set castors and stand	31	12
1 tankard	35	10
1 flat waiter	35	9
1 salver	13	2
1 small waiter	6	3
2 small waiters	15	9
1 punch-strainer	3	2
1 caudle-cup	33	15
1 pair salvers	15	4
1 pair sauce-boats	27	9
2 small saucepans	7	..
1 punch ladle	3	..
12 table spoons	23	15
2 large soup-spoons	11	18
12 table-spoons	24	15
10 table-spoons	18	10
12 custard-spoons	12	5
2 marrow-spoons	3	14
1 pepper-box	2	9
12 tea-spoons	6	11
12 tea-spoons	2	18

The date of the above inventory is 1751. In addition to these articles, it enumerated: 12 silver-
handled knives and forks; 12 dessert ditto; 23 knives
and forks with ivory handles, and 12 dessert ditto.

An early example of the tea-pot is globular. This
form was frequently ornamented with a crest, or coat-
of-arms. Specimens appear on pages 275 and 138.

The former was owned by the Rev. Samuel Johnson, first President of King's College ; and now belongs to his descendants, Mr. and Mrs. William E. Ver Planck. The second, belonging to Mr. and Mrs. Richard Ray, is now owned by their descendant, Mrs. Natalie E. Baylies, of New York. It is noticeable that many tea-pots and tea-kettles of the reigns of George II. and George III. are very simple in design. In these reigns, Louis Quinze designs were also very popular. An example of such a tea-pot, bearing the hall-mark of 1749–'50, appears on page 156. Another tea-pot appears on page 273. The latter belonged to Dr. Matthias Burnet Miller (1749–1792), and was given to his son Judge Morris Smith Miller. This is now owned by his great-granddaughter, Mrs. Wilmot Townsend Cox, of New York. A handsome tea-set, said to date from the middle of the century, belongs to Frederic J. de Peyster, Esq., and appears on page 284.

Silver candlesticks owned by William Walton (1766). See pages 143 and 148.

As a rule, the coffee-pot was slender and taller in form than the tea-pot. Coffee-pots appear on pages 153 and 156. Two coffee-pots of the Louis Quinze period are shown on the latter page. The one on the right with the hall-mark 1758–'9, belonged to James Alexander, father of the Earl of Stirling (see page 76). It has a beautiful pattern of flowers and scroll-work and a border of little bells reminiscent of Chinese ornamentation. The top is shaped like a pine-apple. This piece of silver was buried during the Revolution. It is now owned by Mr. Alexander's descendant, Mrs. Edward Parke Custis Lewis, of Hoboken, N. J. The other coffee-pot, in the same picture, bearing the hall-mark of 1762–'3, is similar in its general design and ornamentation. Another old coffee-pot appears on page 147, and is owned by Mrs. W. W. Shippen of New York.

The cream-jug and sugar-bowl usually matched the tea-pot. Part of a set that originally belonged to Henry Bowers (1747–1800), is shown on page 371. These are now owned by his descendant, Mrs. Wilmot Townsend Cox of New York. Their general shape, with lobes, as well as their square handles and ball feet show that these are early pieces. It may be remarked here that the ball foot upon silver vessels appeared very early in the Seventeenth Century. Upon the same illustration (page 371), is a gravy boat that belonged to Maria Crooke (1721–1794), who was married to Petrus Elmendorph of Kingston. It is owned now by their great-grand-daughter Mrs. Wilmot Townsend Cox. The salt-cellars with their original spoons were owned by John Rutger Bleecker and are now in the possession of Mrs. French Ensor Chadwick. The tankard was owned by Maria Crooke, and the candlestick is one of a pair owned by James Chatham Duane.

Chocolate-pots were much used and sometimes stood on feet. One of quite late date bearing the hall-mark of 1784, and owned by Mrs. Douglas Robinson, of New York, appears on page 352.

The urn is of later date than the tea-kettle. It was generally of a pointed or oval shape. Specimens appear on pages 153 and 147. The former belongs to the de Peyster family ; the second, to Catharine Lynson and is owned by her descendant, Mrs. W. W. Shippen, of New York. In the same illustration is shown a coffee-pot that belonged to Gabriel Ludlow, and coffee-spoons decorated with the heads of jesters. There is also a snuff-box on this plate and an *étui* case once owned by Catharine Rutgers.

A group of silver appears on page 273, together with several small articles. On the left is a sugar-bowl that belonged to a set owned by Maria Livingston and James Duane who were married in 1759. It is now owned by their great-great-grand-daughter, Mrs. French Ensor Chadwick. On the left is a bowl owned by Mrs. Wilmot Townsend Cox. The small salt-cellars that belonged to the Hon. Samuel Jones of New York (1734–1819), are also owned by Mrs. Cox. Between them stands a small filigree bowl, or cup, lined with blue glass, and a spoon. These belonged to Cornelia Harring Jones, wife of the Hon. Samuel Jones and are now owned by her great-great-grand-daughter, Mrs. French Ensor Chadwick.

Silver belonging in the family of the late James de Peyster of New York.

See page 148.

A few examples of plated ware appear on pages 321 and 368. The tea-caddy, snuff-box, dish, and open-work basket on page 368, are owned by Mrs. Alan Hartwell Strong of New Brunswick. On the same illustration are some very interesting card-counters, each stamped with the head of Queen Anne. The little cylindrical box in which these are kept also bears Queen Anne's head.

Silver spoons were to be found in this country from its earliest settlement. The forms of the old spoons were very numerous. The bowls were deep and shallow, egg-shaped, kite-shaped and circular. The stems were round, flat, fluted, spiral, square and worked in many patterns. Sometimes the handle ended in a baluster and square, or hexagonal, engraved button (known as the seal-headed spoon); sometimes in a head or figure. The most famous of those with figures were the Apostles' Spoons, which were always highly prized. They occur frequently in the inventories.

The end of the handle of the Jacobean spoon was broadened, flattened and notched, terminating in three points slightly turned up, and the bowl was a regular oval in shape. This was called the hind's foot spoon and lasted till the end of the reign of Queen Anne.

The new fashion then introduced shows a bowl of a more elongated ellipse; the end of the handle rounded and turned up, and the middle of the stem gradually rising in a high ridge running down to the extremity of the handle. Although other styles were successively introduced, this pattern persisted almost till 1770. About 1750, the shape with which we are familiar to-day, came into fashion. The bowl became more pointed, the deepest part being towards the stem, and the end of the handle was turned down instead of up, as heretofore, while the tongue at the back of the bowl, known as "the rat's tail," was shortened into a drop. This is popularly termed "Old English" pattern. It lasted till the beginning of the Nineteenth Century, when it was supplanted by the pattern known as the "Fiddle Head."

Another spoon that was very popular in Georgian days was used principally for liquor. The figure of a monkey was carried on the handle, and from this it took its name. The monkey-spoon was sometimes found in company with the mourning ring and gloves that were given to the bearers at a funeral. We are told that each of the eight bearers received one at the funeral of Philip Livingston, in 1749.

The marrow-spoon was also of importance. On page 164 several spoons of the period appear with other articles. The small spoons there shown were made by Isaac Hutton, a noted silversmith of Albany, and are now owned by Mrs. F. H. Bosworth of New York. The ladle belonged to Helena Morris and John Rutherford (1782), and are now in the Van Cortlandt Museum. The little spoon in one of the salt-cellars was made by one Forbes, also an American silversmith. On the same plate there is a funeral spoon, now owned by Mrs. Howard Townsend. It was one of the spoons given to the pall-bearers at the funeral of Stephen Van Rensselaer in 1787.

The family silver, especially such as Monteiths tankards, caudle-cups, etc., was sometimes highly prized. We should be astonished that so little old plate has survived if we did not know that our forefathers as a rule had very little veneration for anything that commemorated the fashions of a former day. Gifts from royal personages, such as the pieces of plate given to Governor Burnet by the Electress Sophia for his services to the House of Hanover, or the plate presented to Lord Baltimore by Frederick,

Silver owned by the Cox and Alexander families ; now by Mrs. Edward Parke Custis Lewis. See page 142.

Prince of Wales, were naturally cherished, as were pieces that had sentimental and family associations, but, as a rule, when new fashions came in, much of the old went to the melting-pot.

Before 1700, we find English settlers sending their plate to London to be refashioned according to new styles. Artistic perception had little to do with this custom. Sometimes the new fashions were inferior in beauty to those they supplanted. The mere fact that an article was old-fashioned lowered its value. In the inventories, old and new-fashioned plate are sometimes set down in separate items, the former being valued so much less per ounce. It was a very common custom for a man to send his old cups and salvers to the silversmith when he wanted new tea-pots. A bill rendered by Paul Revere is extant, in which a tea-pot, stand and some spoons came to £15–10–0: against this £8–15–0 was credited for a salver containing 25 oz. of silver. The materials and workmanship were charged separately.

When the stormy days of the Revolution arrived, people who had wealth in the form of plate had reason to congratulate themselves, for in comparison with other goods it was readily removable, and when necessity arose it could be easily hidden. Much was buried, and considerable ingenuity was exercised to keep it out of the clutches of rapacious soldiers. One such case is related in the following letter written by Mrs. Alexander Wallace to Gouverneur Morris, Dec. 28, 1776:

"Mrs. Hugh Wallace is pretty well in health, but very unhappy about her husband being kept so long from her, and what adds to her distress is the very heavy loss she has met with about ten days ago in losing all her plate. She sent it to Mr. Richard Yates last summer at Aquacknock, to be kept there as a place of safety; but upon his leaving that place he had the box which contained the plate put on board a brig, commanded by Capt. Roche, bound to this place. About four miles below Hackinsack the brig was seized by a party of your army, and all the goods taken out. The plate cost upwards of

£1500, this currency. She thinks the gentlemen belonging to the Convention, when they know it belongs to her, will order it to be sent to her immediately, as it would be very hard indeed to send her husband away to Connecticut and allow her property to be plundered. I must request the favour of you to get this affair settled as soon as possible. Enclosed is an inventory of the plate; it was all in one box."

"1 tea urn, 1 epergne, 1 very large bowl, 4 candlesticks, 1 large pudding dish, 2 large salvers, 3 small salvers, 1 large tankard, 1 coffee pot, 1 pitcher, 1 cruet stand, 4 long handled spoons, 4 scalloped spoons, 6 dozen table spoons, 1 dozen dessert spoons, 1 sugar dish, 1 funnel, 1 fish trowel, 6 salts, 2 mustard pots with spoons, 6 skewers, 2 milk pots, 1 tea chest with cannisters, 1 sugar tongs, 4 labels for bottles, 4 tumblers, 4 rummers, 2 black jacks, 1 large soup ladle, 1 marrow spoon."

"Smith Richards, Grocer and Confectioner, at the Sign of the Tea-Canister and Two Sugar Loaves." (1773.)

IV

PEWTER, GLASSWARE, CUTLERY AND BRASS

ALTHOUGH silver was universally employed and highly prized, as we have seen, pewter was a necessity even in the kitchens of the wealthy. Of course, among the lower classes it took the place of silver in all parts of the house. The number of pewterers in New York show how much in demand this ware was. Early in our period, people could buy pewter articles from James Leddel at the Sign of the Platter in Dock Street, but in 1744 he removed to the lower end of Wall Street. Another pewterer was Robert Boyle, who in 1755 lived at the Sign of the Gilt Dish in Dock Street. William Bradford, in Hanover Square, made and sold "all kinds of pewter dishes, tankards, tea-pots, and coffee pots."

In the homes of the rich and middle-class New Yorkers, the place of pewter was in the kitchen, where it was arranged on the dresser as shown in the illustration on page 160. This interesting piece of furniture came from the Skinner house in Perth Amboy. It is now in the kitchen at the Museum of the Colonial Dames at Van Cortlandt. Upon it stand some good pieces of blue and white china.

A great deal of pewter was in use in the early part of the century. Some of the wealthy citizens who owned plate, china, earthenware, copper and brass pos-

159

sessed also many pounds of pewter. In 1705, Captain William Smith's pewter was valued at no less
than £20; and, as Cornelis Jacobs in 1700 had fifty-

Dresser and three-back and four-back chairs ; in the Museum of the New
York Colonial Dames, Van Cortlandt.   See page 159.

six pounds of pewter worth £2, we can form some
idea as to the quantity owned by Captain Smith.
Governor Burnet's pewter was worth as much as
£100–2–6!   Pewter dishes, plates, spoons, tankards
and basins, were constantly imported all through our
period.

Table Furnishings

The kitchen of a New York home frequently contained a mixture of English and Dutch utensils. A portion of the kitchen in the Van Cortlandt house appears on page 49. Although this is now a museum kitchen, a colonial cook would feel perfectly at home here, and would not be embarrassed in preparing a dinner with the utensils provided. Among the miscellaneous kitchen articles imported from time to time, we find "wafel irons," 1750; coffee mills, 1751; sugar-cleavers, 1752; corkscrews, 1752; bread baskets, 1760; polished copper chafing-dishes, 1760; copper tin kitchens with stands, 1763; baskets for plates and baskets for knives, 1765; and after 1760, japanned plate-warmers, "very necessary in this frigid climate." Then, too, we occasionally find some novelties. For example in 1779:

"Joseph Rose at No. 104 Water Street, a few doors east of Peck's Slip has just purchased a quantity of tinware amongst which are a large parcel of Despatches, very suitable for gentlemen of the army or navy and private families: they are worthy of the name of Despatches, as they will cook a beefsteak in about four minutes sufficiently to put on the table, having made the trial myself."

Braziers were numerous, as was natural enough when one remembers the great use of brass hearth-furniture and the various utensils of copper and brass that were used in the kitchen, to say nothing of warming-pans, candlesticks, bird-cages, etc. Most of the artisans came from London, and notwithstanding the fact that articles of brass, iron and copper were constantly being imported, a great deal of work was done in New York. For instance, in 1743:

"John Halden, brasier from London, near the Old Slip Market in New York, makes and sells all sorts of copper and brass kettles, tea kettles, coffee potts, pye pans, warming pans, and all other sorts of copper and brass ware; also sells all sorts of hard metal and pewter wares."

Notwithstanding the increasing demand for grates and stoves as the century advanced, the open wood fire never lost its popularity. We find another brazier as late as 1770, Jacob Wilkins at the Sign of the Brass Andiron and Candlestick, in the Main Street, offering "a few brass fenders plain and open work of different patterns."

An excellent specimen of the brass hearth furniture of the period appears on page 266. Nothing of its history is known except that it belonged to Betty Washington Lewis, the sister of Gen. Washington, and was in her home at *Kenmore*, Fredericksburg, Va. The shovel and tongs are placed on a stand with a marble block grooved for their accommodation. They are owned by Mrs. Edward Parke Custis Lewis of Hoboken, N. J.

Boxes of glass, containing wine-glasses, salt-cellars, sugar-dishes, cream-pots and tumblers were sold by Edward Nicoll, on the New Dock in 1757. An advertisement of 1762 gives a good idea of the variety of articles of this nature that were to be seen on the tables of well-to-do citizens. This new importation consisted of "neat flowered wine and water-glasses, glass salvers, silver top cruet stands, a few neat and small enamelled shank wine glasses, flowered, scalloped and plain decanters, jugs and mugs, salver and pyramids, jelly and silly bub glasses, flowered, plain and enamelled wine glasses, glasses for silver, salts and sweetmeat, poles with spires and glasses, smelling bottles, sconces, tulip and flower glasses of the newest patterns, finger bowls and tumblers of all sorts." Drinking-glasses of the period are shown on page 348.

The larger one, a goblet, standing on a square base, and cut with a festoon for ornament, belonged to Brigadier-General William Livingston (1723–1790), Governor of New Jersey. This is owned by his descendant, Mrs. W. A. Walker of Nyack, New York. The other, a wine-glass, which also has a square base, is owned by Miss Anne Van Cortlandt, of Croton-on-the-Hudson, New York. The two glass salt-cellars in the illustration on page 164, are in the Museum of the New York Colonial Dames at Van Cortlandt. A group of glass articles of this date on page 232 are owned by Mrs. Edward Parke Custis Lewis of "Castle Point," Hoboken, N. J., and consists of decanters, sweetmeat glasses, so frequently mentioned among the importations of the day, four wine-glasses and a tumbler. The five last articles belonged to Gen. Washington and descended to Col. Edward Parke Custis Lewis. The tumbler in the centre is delicately engraved with deer sporting in a forest glade.

Glassware was used in New York very early. It frequently appears in the inventories, but is seldom described. Col. William Smith in 1709, had a case of Venice glasses worth £3 ; a large case and bottles, worth £3, and 3 large cases and bottles, £3. Joseph Bueno (1709), owned 3 glass cups. On Oct.

7, 1754, the following notice appeared in one of the newspapers :

"Thomas Lepper, storekeeper to the Glass House Company, sells all sorts of bottles from 1 quart to 3 gallons and upwards, as also a variety of other glassware. . . . All gentlemen that wants bottles of any size with their names on them . . . may have them made with all expedition."

This advertisement is interesting in connection with the illustration on page 348, upon which are

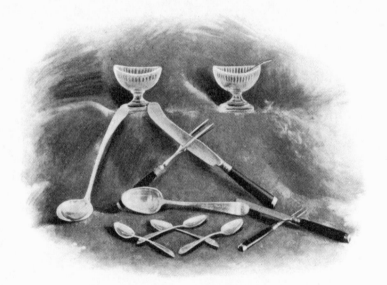

Table furniture of the period.   See pages 155 and 163.

represented three bottles of the kind that Mr. Lepper was able to furnish.   These, however, were made ten years later.   The large bottle on the left bears the name and date "Sidney Breese, 1765."   This is owned by the Museum of the Colonial Dames at Van Cortlandt, New York. The madeira bottle, on the right, has the inscription " F. V. C. 1765" enclosed in a heart raised on the glass, and standing for Frederic Van Cortlandt.

The constant importations of decanters, castors with silver tops, "cruet" or "cruit" stands and "frames," tumblers and glasses for water, wine and beer, cream-jugs, syllabub and sweetmeat glasses, prove how abundantly glass was used on tables. A set of cruets in a plated stand now owned by Mrs. F. H. Bosworth appear on page 321. On the same page is a perforated cake-basket and an old soup-tureen.

The table furniture not only consisted of rich silver, china, and glass, but we note many small articles of luxury, such as nutcrackers in 1750; ivory nutmeg graters, 1753; tea-tongs and punch-strainers in 1759; finger-bowls in 1762; table-bells, 1767; and "steak-tongs and sugar-hatchets" in 1779. The fashionable New Yorkers thought it necessary to keep up with London styles in everything, even in such a small matter as cutlery. Cutlers' advertisements in the papers are many. They always make a point of assuring customers that they have, or will make, articles according to the latest London fashion. We find one Thomas Brown removing in 1743 from Hanover Square to Broad Street, corner of Stone Street, near the Long Bridge; and in 1752 " Edward Andrews, cutler, who served an apprenticeship to the famous Mr. Henry Jones of Sweethings Alley, by the Royal Exchange, London, arrived in this place last week in the *Irene*." He offered to serve people at his

Mahogany knife-boxes and spoon-case, owned by Mrs. F. H. Bosworth.

See page 167.

shop near the Merchant's Coffee House, and "sells and makes all kinds of Cutlery work in the newest fashions now in vogue in London." Among his choice goods, he calls attention to "the noted Constantinople Razor Cases and Strops." Specimens of the black-handled knives and forks ordinarily in use are shown on page 164.

Knives, forks and spoons were kept in shagreen cases, generally green, but sometimes blue; some of the handsomest of these were lined with red velvet from which the ornamental handles of silver, silver gilt, white or green ivory, or decorated china were shown off to advantage. The shagreen case came in very early in the century and continued in use until it was supplanted by the mahogany boxes of the same general shape. If we may judge from the following advertisement the latter began to appear about 1767:

"John Clark, shagreen case maker from London, next door to Mr. Seckell's, Cooper, in Ferry Street, near Peck's Slip Market, makes and sells all sorts of shagreen cases for knives and forks, both in shagreen and mahogany, and cases for Plate, Lady's Dressing-Boxes, Necklaces and Jewel Cases, Buckle cases and Razor Cases of all Sorts."

These cases, of course, contained a series of compartments, as shown in the example to the left on page 166, which also shows one closed and an urn-shaped spoon-case. The knives were placed with their handles upward. Cutlery was constantly changing in fashion; ivory-handled knives and forks, white split bone, buck and black handles were imported in 1750; china-handled knives and forks mounted in silver, in shagreen cases, were sold by Reuben W. Thompson, in Smith's Fly, in 1752; "newest fashioned silver and ebony-handled table knives and forks in shagreen cases," in 1760; camwood-handled knives and three-pronged forks, in 1768; sets of knives, forks, and spoons complete in cases, in 1771; knife, fork, and spoon in a shagreen case for the pocket, in 1771; knife-trays in 1772; knife-cases of fish-skin, in 1774.

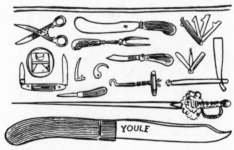

" James Youle, Cutler, at the Sign of the Golden Knife." (1774.)

PART IV

COSTUMES OF MEN

PART IV

COSTUMES OF MEN

_____

I

THE MAN OF FASHION: HIS WIGS AND HATS

THERE is a general impression that people on this side of the water scorned dress and fashion in Colonial times, and that the beau was a type entirely unknown. It is erroneous. The people who frequented the balls and assemblies, routs, tea-gardens and coffee-houses of New York closely followed London fashions.

We shall presently see that men had every opportunity to procure fashionable clothes and to have them cut in the latest European styles. Even more convincing it is to find contemporary evidence of the existence of gallant and smart dress. Although the author of the following contribution to the *New York Mercury*, under date of Jan. 31, 1757, complains of the tyranny of fashion, his protests merely prove how universal was the fop and how unattractive the man who was "out of the mode." Incidentally, he gives us quite a correct idea of the fashions of the time and of what the woman of fashion demanded in the opposite sex. The writer did all he could to please her, even to the adoption of the "fierce Cave Nullo cock," which, of course, is the Kevenhuller hat described on page 178, and resigned himself to the care of a fashionable hairdresser. He writes as follows:

"I am a bachelor turned of thirty, in easy circumstances, and want nothing but a wife to make me as happy as my neighbours.

"I have long admired a young lady who, I can with great propriety, call Miss Modish; though for her unreasonable conduct to me she deserves to have her real name exposed in capitals. She has a mind capable of every improvement and graces of her sex; and were it not for an excessive fondness for gaiety and the reigning amusements of the town, would be unexceptionably lovely.

"To this fair one I have most obsequiously paid my addresses for these last four years; and had I been a *Beau*, or she less a *Belle*, I should undoubtedly long since have succeeded; for fashions, cards and assemblies were the only things in which we did not perfectly agree. But whenever these were the subject of conversation, we were as certainly ruffled and out of temper. On these occasions she would tell me, 'She was astonished I would dispute with her, when every *genteel* person was of her opinion. *That one might be as well out of the world as out of the mode.* For her part, she could never think of managing a man who was so obstinately awkward and impolite, let his other accomplishments be ever so refined. I dressed like a clown, and hardly ever waited on her to a public diversion; and indeed when I did, she was in pain for me, I behaved *so queer.* She had no notion at her age, of sacrificing all the dear pleasures of routs, hops and quadrille for a philosophical husband. No, if I expected to make myself agreeable to her I must learn to *dress gallant* and be *smart.*' Now, truth is, I can't dance, and have an unconquerable aversion to foppery. In order to form me to her taste, Miss Modish has always most obstinately insisted on my complying with every idle fashion that has been introduced since my acquaintance with her, under the severe penalty of *never hoping for her love, if I did not implicitly obey.* This, with infinite reluctance and mortification, I have been under the hard necessity of doing. I remember, when high brimmed hats were in the mode, she insisted on an elevation of my beaver of near half an inch with a fierce Cave Nullo cock. The taste changed, and she would hardly allow me enough to protect my phiz from the inclemency of the weather. My coat, when coatees flourished, was reduced to the size of a dwarf's, and then again increased to the longitude of a surtout. The cuffs in the winter were made open, for the benefit of taking in the cool north weather; in the summer again they were close, to prevent the advantage of the refreshing breeze. In the summer, I was smothered with a double cravat: in the winter, relieved again with a single cambric neckcloth. It would be tedious to repeat the many surprising and ridiculous changes I underwent in the outward man; let it suffice to observe that my wigs, ruffles, shoes, and every little particular, not excepting my breeches, have shared the same unaccountable metamorphosis, all which grievous foppery, my excessive fondness

Miniature of Lewis Morris (1641– 1746), owned by Mrs. Ostrander. See page 176.

for her made me suffer with Christian resignation; but at last she has fairly exhausted my patience, and we are now come to an open rupture, the occasion of which was this: We unhappily fell into the old topic of my want of taste and breeding. '*You will always,*' says she, '*be an old-fashioned creature.*' (I had unluckily called her *My dear*). 'Lord, can't you take pattern after Mr. Foppington? How happy must a lady be in such an admirer! He's always easy and good-humoured, and pays the finest compliments of any gentleman in the universe! How elegantly he dresses! And then he sings like an angel and dances to perfection; and as for his hair, I never saw anything so exquisitely fine. Surely the hair is the most valuable part of a man!'

"From this teasing introduction, she took occasion to insist on my wearing my hair; observing that I could not refuse it, since I saw how pleasing it would be to her. I used all the arguments I could to divert her from this unreasonable request; but she peremptorily declared she would never speak to me again if I denied her so small a favour; it was an insult on the prerogative of her sex and a convincing proof that I neither loved her, nor merited her esteem. I remonstrated, in vain, that even if I was inclined to *play the fool*, and put my head, which as it happened I could not well spare, into the hands of Monsieur Piermont, I was well assured that all the skill and industry of that eminent artist would never change it from its native red, or form a single curl, for that ever since I was six years old, it had been condemned to be close shorn, as incapable of affording a creditable covering to my pericranium. In a passion she desired never to see me more: she would not put up with such contradictions in any gentleman who pretended to be her admirer."

The dressing-table of the gentleman of the period was equipped with every article of the toilet known to-day, and with a vast array of cosmetics, essences, oils, butters, pomatums and powders, with which the most fashionable man of the present day is unfamiliar. The latter, however, would not scorn "the complete set of shaving utensils in shagreen cases," "the shagreen two and four-hole razor cases completely filled," that could be bought from James Wilmot at the Golden Fleece, Hanover Square, nor the "complete shaving equipages, holding razors, scissors, hones, penknives, combs, oil-bottle, brush and soap box, with places for paper, pens and ink." These were made of japanned ware, straw, red, or blue Morocco, or shagreen. "Fish-skin razor cases" were also to be had, as well as "nail nippers," "neat Morocco tweese cases," and boxes for wigs, wig-ribbons, cravats, hats, etc.

Dressing was as serious an occupation for men as for women. The man of fashion spent a great deal of time upon his toilet and then upon his self-adornment, and what was true of the beau, was, to a great extent, true of every man of affluence and position. The arrangement of the wig alone consumed a great amount of time ; for the gentlemen, unlike the ladies, had their hair dressed every day. Some of them put their curls up in papers at night and used curling-tongs the next day. The barber, of course, was re-quired, for what man could have arranged upon his own head any one of the varieties in fashion in 1753, such as the pigeon's wing, the comet, the cauliflower, the royal bird, the staircase, the ladder, the brush, the wild boar's back, the temple, the rhinoceros, the corded wolf's paw, Count Saxe's mode, the she-dragon, the rose, the crutch, the negligent, the chan-cellor, the cut-bob, the long bob, the half natural, the chain-buckle, the corded buckle, the detached buckle, the Jansenist bob, the drop wig, the snail back, the spinach seed, and the artichoke ?

On Oct. 22, 1753, John Bury, at the Crown and Shears, in Beaver Street, announced that he had im-ported "a neat assortment of hairs of all sorts for perukes," and in 1754, we read :

175

"This is to inform all Gentlemen and Ladies who have honoured Mr. David Cox with their custom that the same business is now carried on at the same shop next door to the Kings Arms Tavern and opposite the Royal Exchange, by Timothy Powell, hair-curler and peruke-maker from London, who has just imported an assortment of English hairs; where all Gentlemen who are pleased to favour me with their orders, may have all sorts of perukes, viz. Tyes, bags, drest or cut bobs at the most reasonable rates and made in the genteelest and newest fashion. . . .

"N. B. Ladies Tates and towers made in the genteelest and newest manner."

Previous to this date, the wigs had been the full-bottomed, the tie, or Ramilies, the bag and the bob wigs, major and minor. The full-bottomed is that of the flowing curls familiar since the days of William and Mary and Queen Anne, and which is worn by Col. Lewis Morris on page 173. This was out of fashion by 1739.

The Ramilies,* invented by some enterprising barber after the Battle of Ramilies (May 23, 1706), consisted of a bushy head, well powdered, arranged at the back in a braided pig-tail or *queue*, and tied at the top with a large bow of ribbon and at the bottom with a smaller one. The bag-wig is thought to have had its origin with the French servants who tied up their hair when they were doing their work.

Gentlemen's bags were always of silk or satin. This style was much affected by doctors and lawyers.

About 1774 it was said that a small man's shoulders were "perfectly covered with black satin." The

---

* A good example of the Ramilies wig occurs in Hogarth's *Modern Midnight Conversation* and *Taste in High Life in the Year 1742*.

bob wig was less ornate, being an imitation of the real head of hair, and it was worn by the common people; the major bob had several rows of curls.

During the reigns of George II. and George III., the bag and the Ramilies were, perhaps, the favourite wigs, but there was still another,—" the pigeon winged toupee," mentioned in 1753, which developed into the extraordinary Macaroni toupee, that was brushed erect about a foot above the forehead and plastered with pomatum. It was ornamented with large curls at either side and gathered at the back into a large club-shaped knot that rested on the back of the neck.

We may be certain that all of these styles were worn in New York, by glancing at a few advertisements. In 1750, we find the following:

" This is to acquaint the Publick, that there is lately arrived from London, the Wonder of the World, an honest Barber and Peruke-Maker, who might have worked for the King if his Majesty would have employ'd him: It was not for the Want of Money that he came here, for he had enough of that at Home; nor for the Want of Business, that he advertises himself. But to acquaint the Gentlemen and Ladies That such a Person is now in town living near Rosemary Lane, where Gentlemen and Ladies may be supplied with the Goods as follows, viz., Tyes, Full Bottoms, Majors, Spencers, Fox Tails, Ramalies, Tucks, Cuts and Bob Perukes; also Ladies Tatematongues and Towers, after the Manner that is now worn at Court. By their humble and obedient Servant, John Still."

Passing by many other eminent " artists " in the hair-dressing line, we may note the styles of 1761:

" To be sold at Duthie's London Peruke Warehouse all sorts of Perukes ready made of the newest Fashions, at the lowest prices that can be afforded by any one of the Business that does Justice to his Customers, and warranted to be of as

good Hairs and as good Work as any in America. Also Ladies'
Teatts, Bandoas for the Hair, and Bags of the newest Fashion,
Roapeats, Ramelleas, and hard and soft Pomatum, false Ques
and many other Articles necessary in that Way."

We cannot take leave of the wig without describing the cocked hat, which remained in fashion until
1789. There were many varieties : indeed, a man
was always known by the cock of his hat. The most
fashionable was the one trimmed with gold lace and
feathers ; but hardly less so was the hat worn with
the Ramilies wig and known as the " Ramilies cock."
A plainer one accorded with the bag-wig, while the
" Kevenhuller," extremely large and aggressive and
decorated with a cockade, was worn by officers and
gentlemen swaggerers :

> " When Anna ruled and Kevenhuller fought,
> The hat its title from the hero caught."

It long continued popular. The Nivernois was small,
as was that affected by the Macaroni, and it had a
small crown, to which small flaps were attached. In
addition to these varieties, there was also a folding
theatre hat. Hats were round in 1770, and in 1772
are described as " rising behind and falling before."

New Yorkers were just as fastidious about their
head-gear as Londoners. Castor and felt hats, fine
castor hats and gold laced hats were imported in great
numbers, and in 1762 there was a special invoice of
" gentlemen's superfine laced and plain hats dressed
and cock'd by the most fashionable hatter in England." In addition to these, we find men's velvet
caps, single and double striped worsted caps, flowered
and plain scarlet caps, men and boys' castor and felt

hats, men's velvet morning caps, and velvet hunting caps constantly among the importations.

After the gentleman's hair was dressed and thoroughly sprinkled with grey or blue powder, heavily scented, there were other difficult tasks to perform.

Silver tankard, paste knee-buckles, gold seals, walking-stick and coat buttons, belonging to William Beekman; and a piece of rose-coloured brocade. See pages 137, 183 and 193.

One of these was the tying of his Barcelona or India muslin cravat, the adjusting of his stock and stock buckle, or the arrangement of his "solitaire,"—a loose black ribbon fastened to the bag-wig and brought around the neck in front. After scenting his plain or flowered silk handkerchief with some strong perfume, preferably musk, filling his snuff-box, fastening his sword to his side and taking his walking-stick or cane in his hand, he would tuck his beaver under his arm and sally forth to Ranelagh or Vauxhall Gardens, to a public vendue, to pay a social call, to meet his friends at one of the coffee-houses, to look after his business affairs, or to make some purchases, if he had read some such tempting notice as :

" Rivington and Brown, in Hanover Square, have this day imported from London in the ships *Manchester* and *Edward*, Gentlemens laced and plain hats, dress'd and cock'd by the most fashionable hatter in England ; genteel boots, spur leathers, and doe-skin boot straps with handsome buckles. The most beautiful double gilt pinchbeck buckles for shoes and knees ; paper snuff-boxes finely painted and gilt ; best Strasburg snuff and rappee ; fine high dried snuff, commonly called Black Guard ; shaving equipage containing razors, scissars, penknives, combs, hones, oil bottle, brush and soap box, with places for paper, pens and ink ; elegant tooth-pick cases with best Lisbon tooth picks. . . . A choice assortment of jewelry, paste buckles, earrings, solitairs, necklaces, stay-hooks, gold rings, seals, broaches, gold buttons, ettwees, etc."

" Nesbitt Deane, Hats." (1774.)

II

THE CLOTHES MEN WORE

AND now, if it be asked how our exquisite, who, until 1749, was known as a "Fribble," was dressed, we shall have to note that about 1727–1730 he wore black velvet breeches, a Ramilies wig, a coat that fitted very smartly and was buttoned tightly at the waist, trimmed with lace, and open from the neck to the waist to show the lace ruffles beneath it. He had an array of buttons, his sleeve was finished with a deep cuff, and his wrists were adorned with ruffles. His waistcoat was long, and adorned with buttons and flaps. His shoes were gay with red heels, his silk stockings had gold clocks, his hat was a cocked beaver, and he wore a sword and carried a cane decorated with tassels.

The clothes that Gov. Montgomerie wore conformed to the above in every detail. Among them were cambric ruffled shirts, dimity vests, a scarlet coat and breeches trimmed with gold lace, a cloth suit with open silver lace, silk stockings with clocks, a gold-headed cane, and several wigs.

A few years later, the coat had grown longer, reaching to the calf of the leg, fitting as tightly at the waist as ever, and just as profusely adorned with buttons. The cuff, now somewhat smaller at the wrist, reached to the elbow, and a broad collar turned over and lay low upon the shoulders. The coat was still open, showing the ruffle or frill of the shirt.

About 1744, there was a slight change. The coat was no longer laced, although a plain band of lace was retained upon the still ample waistcoat. The skirts of the coat were lined with stiff buckram, or canvas, and stood out in rigid folds, and still fell below the knee. The stockings were drawn over the knee and just met the breeches, ornamented as before with glittering buckles. In 1753, a writer exclaimed :

"What gentleman now rolls his stockings? or lets his breeches cover the cap of his knee? Who suffers his coat-skirts to hang low enough to hide his thighs? or, who dare appear now with high-topped gloves? Are not, even on the stage, *full bottoms* discouraged? Nay, a Brigadier is as unseemly; the *scratch* usurps the throne of *long-bobs*, and a *tye-wig* is banished for a *pigeon-winged toupee*. But the hats—the hats, gentlemen, suffer most. Is not the *Dettingen cock* forgotten? the noble *Kevenhuller* discouraged? Are not hats brought down to caps? and ladies, who will exceed in extremes, disdain to wear caps at all."

At the beginning of George III.'s reign, our beau decorated his coat and waistcoat with a profusion of lace, and wore a small black cravat. Otherwise, his costume suffered no change. The costume of 1766 is well hinted at in Anstey's *New Bath Guide*, when Simkin dresses himself in the latest fashion. He writes home :

"For I ride in a chair, with my hands in a muff,
And have bought a silk coat and embroidered the cuff;
But the weather was cold, and the coat it was thin,
So the tailor advised me to line it with skin :
But what with my Nivernois' hat can compare
Bag-wig, and laced ruffles, and black solitaire?

And what can a man of true fashion denote,
Like an ell of good riband tyed under the throat?
My buckles and box are in exquisite taste,
The one is of paper, the other of paste."

The next and last change was a violent one. In 1770, the Macaroni appeared, whose style of head dress we have already described. He cut his coat much shorter and left it unfastened to show his waistcoat, also shortened till it reached the waist only. His two watches, with their dangling seals, hung from his pockets; and a large white neckerchief was tied in a full bow beneath his chin. The turnover collar of his coat was small. The latter fitted snugly and was ornamented with lace or braid, embroidery, frogs and sometimes tassels. His tight breeches of striped or spotted silk reached to the knee and were tied with bunches of ribbons or strings. Small paste or diamond buckles adorned

William Beekman (1725–1795). From a portrait in possession of the Beekman family. See page 193.

his shoes, and his stockings, of course, were of silk. Upon his enormous toupee, was perched a tiny hat, which he removed with his cane when necessary. The latter was decorated with tassels. A sword also dangled at his side.

He was a very curious object and did not escape caricatures and lampoons of all kinds. The *Oxford Magazine* for 1770 said : " A kind of animal, neither male nor female, lately started up amongst us. It is called a *Macaroni.* It talks without meaning, it smiles without pleasantry, it eats without appetite, it rides without exercise." The type originated about 1770, when a number of fashionable young Englishmen who had made the "Grand Tour," formed themselves, on their return, into a club, which they named in honour of Italy's favourite dish. From the Macaroni Club they took their name, and they carried extravagance in fashion, in dress, and in manner to the verge of absurdity. In 1772–'3, they altered their costume slightly, combing their hair still higher above their foreheads in an oval shape, with large curls above each ear. They also wore knots of flowers upon their breasts.

Horace Walpole noticed them in 1772, fathering them upon Lord Clive. " Lord Chatham," he wrote, " begot the East India Company, the East India Company begot Lord Clive, and Lord Clive begot the Macaronis ; and they begot poverty ; and all the race are still living." Under date of Feb. 17, 1773, he said : " A winter without politics . . . . even our Macaronis entertain the town with nothing but new dresses and the size of their nosegays. They have lost all their money and exhausted their credit and can no longer game for twenty thousand pounds a night."

For a few years, everything was *à la Macaroni*, and the term was as familiar in New York as in Lon-

184

don. In September, 1771, we even find "The Macaroni Purse for £100" being run for by Mr. De Lancey's *Lath* and Mr. Waters's *Liberty*. The word was also adopted here as a *nom de plume*. The name is particularly interesting to Americans on account of the song beginning:

> "Nankee Doodle came to town
> Upon his little pony,
> Stuck a feather in his hat
> And called it Macaroni."

The story that this popular song is of Cromwellian origin is scorned by the best authorities on old English ballads, who hold that the word Macaroni establishes the date of the lines when the derisive words had peculiar significance, for the Macaroni was then a familiar figure.

Gentlemen in New York had every opportunity to keep up with changes in fashions. The tailors were a numerous body. In 1750, "Simon Smith, Taylor, from London, living at his shop at Mr. Joseph Delaplain's, joiner, in Smith's Fly, near the Fly Market, makes all sorts of Mens and Boy's Cloaths, lac'd or plain, likewise Ladies Habits and Riding Josephs in the newest Fashion."

In 1751, Joseph Reed, Taylor, from London, removed from Depuyster's Street to the Sign of the Blue Ball in Wall Street, and in the same year "William Anderson, Taylor, makes all sorts of laced or plain Cloaths in the newest Fashion as in London." In 1771, Ennis Graham is selling clouded silk waistcoat patterns richly embroidered and spangled, gold spangled frogs for clothes and "macaroni velvet."

Fashionable tailors in large numbers advertised clothes of costly and beautiful materials in large quantities, but space will not allow further quotations. In 1775, William Thorne gives a price list of the most sumptuous dress of the day. From this we learn that a plain suit superfine cloth cost £8–10–0; a half trimmed ditto, £9–0–0; full drest ditto, £10–0–0; coat and waistcoat, superfine cloth, £6–15–0; a suit best velvet, any colour, lined with satin, £38–0–0; suit figured Manchester velvet, £15–10–0; suit rateen trimmed with feather velvet and gold buttons, £21–0–0; pair silk velveret breeches, £2–0–0; single coat, superfine cloth, £5–0–0; plain suit second best cloth, £7–0–0; coat and waistcoat, ditto, £5–5–0; surtout coat, best Bath beaver, £2–15–0; plain cloth suit livery, £5–16–0; ditto, with shag breeches, £7–0–0; thickset frock and waistcoat, £3–16–0; and livery surtout coat, £3–16–0.

"To be Sold or Let." (1767.)

III

COATS, BUTTONS, SHOES AND GLOVES

HAVING spoken of fashions and of the tailors who made every effort to secure them promptly, a few specific examples of what some individuals actually owned will prove of interest. We can hardly wonder that the owner of the coat described below as lost in 1746 was anxious to recover it :

"Last night was taken out of a house in this city, supposed by a Mistake, a blue Broadcloth coat, with light blue silk frogs on it, with a double cape and silver Hooks and Eyes, the Binding on the right side is much wore." Ten shillings is offered and no questions asked.

In 1760 and 1763, we find two other announcements of stolen clothes that are descriptive of the articles. The first reads :

"Stolen from Jonathan Grimes of Second River in New Jersey, supposed by an Irishman named John Smith, a few days ago the following articles, viz. A light coloured Broad cloth coat with blue Lining, white buttons and button holes, two pair of Pumps, one pair of blue serge Breeches with white Lining, a white Shirt and a pair of large Brass Buckles." £3 reward is offered for the thief.

The second plea is as follows :

"Lent to a gentleman some time ago, a blue cloth surtout coat with metal buttons. As the coat has not been returned, it is supposed the gentleman forgot where he had it. This is to desire the gentleman to send it to John Crawley's, at the

New York Arms, whose property it is and it will be received with thanks."

The surtout, mentioned in the above advertisement, had been a very fashionable garment for some time. The hard-hearted Miss Modish, as we have seen, compelled her admirer to adopt one. The fashionable surtout that was worn in 1762–'3, had four flaps on each side called "dog's ears." The long cloak had not been abolished, however, even if the great-coat had won its way into popular favour. In 1760, the owner of one thus advertised its loss :

"Dropped from behind a Sleigh on 22 of December, between the hours of ten and eleven at Night from Windmill House to the Fly, a large Spanish Cloak of brown Camblet lined with green Bays, with a large Hood of the same almost ripped off, and ripped at the Seam on the right Shoulder. Whoever has found said Cloak, and will bring it to the Printer hereof, or to Mr. David Cox, Peruke-Maker, in Broad Street shall receive sixteen shillings reward."

In 1764, a gentleman lost "a brown camblet cloak lined with red baize ;" and in 1765, another gentleman, "a large Spanish brown Camblet cloak lined with Green Baize, with a large Cap to it," for which he offered four dollars reward.

The wardrobe of an ordinary New York gentleman about 1740 consisted of a suit of blue broadcloth trimmed with silver, a suit of black broadcloth, a suit of camlet trimmed with silver, a fustian coat and breeches, a green coat and breeches, a new broadcloth trimmed with gold, three pairs of silk stockings, five pairs of worsted stockings, a pair of silver shoe and stock-buckles, a pair of brass knee-buckles, and three wigs. This was not excessive. Handsomer costumes were sold at Moore and Lynsen's Vendue House in 1764, such as a suit of superfine white broadcloth trimmed with gold; a scarlet vest laced with gold; a suit of silk trimmed with silver; and a suit of superfine blue "trimmed with gold vellum holes."

On page 195 is shown a fashionable costume of about 1760, worn by Richard Ray of New York. The coat and trousers are of bluish green, with gold buttons, the waistcoat is white satin trimmed with gold lace. The stock, neckcloth and sleeve-ruffles are

White silk waistcoat embroidered in colours. See page 193.

white. The portrait is owned by Miss Ellen King.

We may now turn to the unpublished inventory of the belongings of an officer in the Royal Americans,—Capt. T. Parker of the Fourth Battalion, who died in Martinique in 1762. He was the brother of Elisha Parker, mentioned on pages 302 and 303. This list includes: " 1 red surtout coat; 4 cloath waistcoats; 6 pair breeches; 2 pair gloves; 1 pair leggins; 1 pair mackisins; 2 plain hats; 1 blue surtout; 1 muff; 1 pair silver shoe buckles; 29 shirts; 2 pairs linen

drawers; 18 nightcaps; 4 handkerchiefs; 6 white
linen waistcoats; 2 flannel waistcoats; 5 pairs silk
stockings; 13 cotton stockings; 13 worsted stockings; ½ doz. waistcoat buttons; 3 doz. white buttons;
1 sword belt; 1 pair leather gloves; 1 sash; 1 gorget;
1 silver mounted sword; 1 clothes brush; 2 shaving-
boxes, and 1 shaving-brush."

And now let us pause to examine some of the
more expensive materials that were imported by and
for the tailors, omitting all such goods as fustians,
camlets, friezes, sateens, serges, etc. It will be noticed that the button was of great importance, as it
formed a trimming for coat and waistcoat, especially
during the reign of George III., who was himself so
fond of making buttons that he was laughed at in a
satire called *The Button Maker's Jest-Book.* "Vel-
lum-holes" were also used for decoration.

We find among the lists: New fashion buttons
and mohair, 1732; silk camlets with silk and hair
buttons to suit, striped linsey coats, Scotch plaid,
snake-skin coatings, light and cloth-coloured sarsenet,
silk and hair buttons, gilt buttons, 1743; worsted
plad water'd grograms, scarf buttons, 1745; fine embroidered waistcoats, metal and gilt buttons, new
fashioned coat and waistcoat buttons, fine silk and
worsted patterns for waistcoats and breeches, silk and
worsted waistcoats and breeches pieces, mens knit
waistcoats, black and white stript lutestrings, and
Turky Tabby buckrams, and breast and shirt metal
buttons, 1750; black silk knit waistcoats and breeches,
scarlet and black knit worsted waistcoats and breeches,
Saxon green knit waistcoats, 1751; an assortment of

yellow and white metal buttons, 1752; gold and silver
wire and mohair buttons, and death's head black vest
buttons, 1754; coloured thread, metal, worsted, and
death's head buttons, nankeens and breeches patterns,

Eighteenth century shoe, stock, and knee buckles, of gold and silver set
with paste; watches, chatelaines, buttons and fobs; originals in the
Museum for the Art of Decoration, Cooper Union. See page 254.

damask of sundry sorts for vests, black, blue, white, scarlet and crimson silk and worsted breeches patterns, black, blue and cloth coloured best Manchester velvet, Manchester velvet shapes for vests, gilt and plated buttons, silk twist buttons, gold and silver lace, silk and hair grogram and corded tabby, blue and crimson Genoa velvet, and remnants of velvet of all colours for caps and collars of coats, 1760; gold and silver buttons, best London gilt and plate buttons; three cord silk twist buttons, Prussian mold and basket buttons, 1760; crimson, scarlet and black silk breeches patterns, 1761; basket and plain gilt buttons, silk breeches patterns, 1762; plaited basket coat and vest buttons, 1764; blue and scarlet new-fashioned Bath coating, newest fashion gold, silver and metal, scarf, basket, death's head, mohair and other buttons fit for slop shops, horsehair buttons and other trimming for hatters, gold and silver shoulder knots, gold and silver shoulder straps, knee garters, blue, black, buff, crimson, scarlet and cloth coloured worsted breeches patterns, blue, black, buff, crimson, scarlet and cloth coloured silk breeches patterns, corded tabbies for men's vests, 1767; silk clouded vest patterns richly embroidered and spangled, gold spangled frogs for clothes, 1771; and royal ribbed and Macaroni velvet, feather velvet, figured Manchester velvet, 1775. In 1773, John Laboyteaux, tailor, promised "Any gentleman that chooses to have buttons made of the same cloth can have them worked with purl and spangles with any sprig or flower that they choose, as neat as those made in London." A handsome white silk waistcoat embroidered in colours appears on page 189. It belonged to a Col. John Brown who died in 1781.

Steel buttons are shown on page 179. These belonged to William Beekman and were the same that trim the waistcoat he wears in his portrait on page 183. It will be noticed that he carries his cocked hat under his arm in the fashionable style. The shoes of the men, generally speaking, were like the women's, —with high heels, high vamp and buckles on the instep. In 1753, the beau wore :

> " A pair of smart pumps made up of grained leather,
> So thin he can't venture to tread on a feather ;
> His buckles like diamonds must glitter and shine—
> Should they cost fifty pounds they would not be too fine."

All through our period, there were importations of fine stitched pumps, neat channelled boots and pumps, turned pumps ; and double and single channelled pumps, and in 1763, Alexander Montgomery, at the Fly Market, next door to Mr. Brovort's, opposite to Mrs. Rutgers, offered "a parcel of greased leather double and single channelled pumps, stitched high heeled shoes and pumps of the very best sort, from fourteen shillings to sixteen shillings per pair."

The buckle was the important ornament of the shoe : these were of diamonds, paste, gold, silver, open-worked polished steel, pinchbeck, or black. The high top-boot with its upper part of light leather, was worn by huntsmen, and the dashing bucks and dandies of the day often appeared in them. Of course, spurs were fixed to them. These boots were worn by the officers, for, like the Kevenhuller cocked hat, they were distinctly military. There were numerous shoemakers in New York, but probably not very many who had the courage to expose their patrons, as one of them does in 1749 :

" This is to give notice to the person who calls himself a gentleman of the city of New York, and who was pleased to send me so many messages concerning the making of his extraordinary shoes, that they are now done and finished, therefore pray him to come (tho' not without money) and fetch them, for as I have known him a bad paymaster some years, do not care now leather is dear, to let them go without, and as they are made the one larger than the other, on account of his sore foot, beg that he would not let them lie on my hands, lest I expose him more publicly."

Stockings were invariably of silk with clocks, and until the last years of George II. were rolled beneath the knee and kept in place by the garter and knee-buckles, which were similar to the shoe-buckles, but larger. Knee-garters were of silk. Cloth-coloured knee-garters appeared in 1760, and we even find among the goods that Mr. Stuyvesant advertised for sale in 1764 "ladies' and gentlemen's silk garters with mottoes." Large bunches of ribbons, or strings, decorated the knees of the Macaroni.

The shirt was always of fine linen, or cambric, and was frequently trimmed with a frill when a small cravat was worn. During some seasons the black solitaire that was fastened to the bag-wig was preferred ; at others, a stock and stock-buckle ; and, finally, in the Macaroni period, the style was to wrap oneself in a large neckerchief, which was tied in a bow under the chin. Specimen stock, knee and shoe-buckles appear on page 191 ; and a pair of paste knee buckles on page 179.

Ruffles always framed the wrists and these were often of rich lace. "Gentlemen's ruffles of blond lace" were sold by Nicholas Stuyvesant in 1764.

There were many varieties of handkerchiefs, such as plain and flowered, and those made of various kinds of silk. We meet with both Barcelona handkerchiefs and cravats.

Among the varieties of gloves we may note: "Men's and boys glazed kid and lamb, unbound and ribbon bound gloves" and "men's coloured welted mittens," 1751; "men's black and white silk gloves, black and white buck, shammy, and wash leather, shammy and best buckskin gloves," 1769.

Portrait of Richard Ray, painted about 1760. See page 189.

The jewelry consisted of knee, shoe, and stock buckles, watches with a bunch of seals (the Macaroni wore two watches) and rings. The men, of course, wore swords, and carried canes and walking-sticks and often umbrellas. The canes and walking-sticks were gold, silver, or ivory-headed, and in 1745 sometimes had small compasses fixed upon them. An ivory headed walking-stick that belonged to William Beekman appears on page 179, and other examples, with a sword, on page 263. "Umbrelloes of all sorts" were imported in 1761 by John Hammersly and Company, near the Coenties Market, and in 1764 silk umbrellas were advertised.

The pocket-book was of red Morocco with silver clasps, such as the one lost at the Play House in 1761, or of shagreen with silver or pinchbeck clasps. Frequently in the pocket an essence-bottle was carried, and, of course, the snuff-box. The latter was of every variety : gold or silver, plain, chased or jewelled, set with precious or semi-precious stones, or paste, of tortoiseshell, of china painted and enamelled, and of French paper. A very handsome one was described on Dec. 5, 1748, as "a silver snuff box of an oval figure ; the lid, mother-of-pearl, with a shell carved upon it." A collection of tortoiseshell-boxes appears on page 376.

Although the period under review was essentially one of splendid attire and ceremonial robes, yet in New York, a democratic tendency towards a neglect of form was sometimes observable. As early as 1747, a writer who calls himself Thomas Trim speaks of the great uneasiness he feels when he observes the contempt with which the people sometimes treat their elective magistrates. The fault he said lay entirely with the latter, because they did not maintain the dignity of their office, but consorted with the lowest of the people. Another cause that contributed to the contempt of Corporation Magistrates was the robes they wore in the distribution of justice. Thomas Trim went on to say :

"To see an alderman sit or stand in the seat of Justice, and award the payment of 5s 6d to a person of his Ward that comes to him for relief, in the pompous robe of a greasy woollen cap and a tettered Banjam jacket, must certainly command the greatest respect, both to their knowledge and good manners. Yet I have seen one of these robed magistrates vouchsafe to powder his wig and put it on, without quitting his Banjam, to sup with one of the Ward upon the profits of his daily labour, provided the feast was graced with some good oysters, a pipe of tobacco and a mug of strong beer. I am not for becoming a slave to the fashion, or making dress the whole business of my life; though at the same time, I think every person that appears in public, clothed in authority, should be decent and clean. The people in general love show, and always pay a greater regard to a magistrate in his proper robes than when he thinks proper to appear in the dress of a smith, mason, or carpenter. I will venture to affirm, no magistrate ever lost a vote by putting on a clean shirt when he was dirty, or clothing the seat of his brain with a powdered wig instead of a dirty cap, or even by keeping of good Company."

The ship *Hope*. (1767.)